JUSTICE
AT THE
MARGINS
OF WAR

JUSTICE AT THE MARGINS OF WAR

THE ETHICS OF ESPIONAGE AND GRAY ZONE OPERATIONS

Edited by Edward Barrett

McCain Conference,
United States Naval Academy
2021

Naval Institute Press
Annapolis, Maryland

The 2021 McCain Conference and this resulting edited volume
were generously supported by Bloomberg Philanthropies.

Naval Institute Press
291 Wood Road
Annapolis, MD 21402

© 2023 by Edward Barrett
All rights reserved. No part of this book may be reproduced or utilized in any form or by any means, electronic or mechanical, including photocopying and recording, or by any information storage and retrieval system, without permission in writing from the publisher.

Library of Congress Cataloging-in-Publication Data
Names: Barrett, Edward, 1961– editor.
Title: Justice at the margins of war : the ethics of espionage and gray zone operations / edited by Edward Barrett.
Identifiers: LCCN 2023007194 | ISBN 9781682472095 (paperback)
Subjects: LCSH: Espionage--Moral and ethical aspects. | Military intelligence--Moral and ethical aspects. | Intelligence service--Moral and ethical aspects.
Classification: LCC JF1525.I6 J87 2023 | DDC 327.12--dc23/eng/20230307
LC record available at https://lccn.loc.gov/2023007194

♾ Print editions meet the requirements of ANSI/NISO z39.48-1992 (Permanence of Paper).
Printed in the United States of America.

9 8 7 6 5 4 3 2 1

CONTENTS

PREFACE	*Edward Barrett*	vii
Chapter 1	An Interview with Mr. Michael Morell, Former Deputy and Acting Director of the Central Intelligence Agency *Conducted by Mitt Regan & Edward Barrett*	3
Chapter 2	The Ethics of Espionage *Cécile Fabre*	20
Chapter 3	A Contractualist Framework for Intelligence Ethics *Michael Skerker*	27
Chapter 4	The Torture Debate *David Luban*	35
Chapter 5	Technology and the Moral Limits of Intelligence Collection *C. Anthony Pfaff*	45
Chapter 6	Ethical Reflections on Human Intelligence (HUMINT) Gathering *Professor Sir David Omand*	56
Chapter 7	Secrecy, Deception, and Covert Action *Mitt Regan*	68
Chapter 8	*Jus Ad Vim* and Measures Short of War *Helen Frowe*	83
Chapter 9	An Ethical Framework for Grey Zone Responses *Edward Barrett*	92
Chapter 10	Truth-Telling during War: The Ethics of Propaganda and Media Warfare *Michael L. Gross*	98
Chapter 11	Using Hostages in the Grey Zone: An Ethical Assessment *Tamar Meisels*	115
Chapter 12	The Evolution of Norms in Cyber Warfare: From Stuxnet to Solar Winds *George Lucas*	129
Chapter 13	The Ethics of Grey Zone Operations: Election Manipulation *Jens Ohlin*	145
Chapter 14	Lawfare in the Grey Zone *Orde Kittrie*	153
CONTRIBUTORS		163

PREFACE
Edward Barrett

This volume is a fruit of the 2021 McCain Conference at the United States Naval Academy and fills two important gaps in the literature on the ethics of national security affairs.

First, while thinking about the justice of warfare is highly developed, justifications of intelligence activities—which can involve lying, manipulation, coercion, stealing, and even killing in order to obtain and defend information—are relatively limited and often conflicting.[1] At least three ways of justifying these harmful activities exist. One school of thought argues that the logic of the rights-based just war criteria is also applicable to espionage, and that any harm associated with obtaining or defending secrets must be preceded by actual or forthcoming wrongdoing—the very thing that espionage is often attempting to establish. Another theory insists that spying is a "game" in which participants hypothetically consent or tactily contract to abide by certain rules, which include reciprocal permissions to harm each other in various ways. A third school justifies harmful intelligence activities simply as necessary means to attaining the good end of securing the rights of one's citizens, to whom one has special obligations. Predictably these three justifications—rights forfeiture, rights waiver, and necessary/lesser evil, respectively—can result in very different permissions when applied to agent recruitment, human and technical methods of espionage and counterintelligence, interrogational torture, analysis, covert action, sabotage, and assassination.[2]

Second, ethical work on interstate conflict occurring in a "grey zone" between war and peace has only just begun. Like spying, grey zone operations—the use of low-level lethal and sublethal means to weaken others economically, militarily, culturally, ideologically, socially, and politically—are not new. But the intensity and significance of this realm of competition has increased in past decades for at least three reasons. First, Operation Desert Storm in 1991 reduced the attractiveness of conventionally challenging the United States. It's no coincidence that eight years later (and two years before China joined the WTO), two People's Liberation Army colonels outlined an "unrestricted warfare" strategy emphasizing non military means to weaken other states.[3] Second, technological developments such as computers and the internet have magnified vulnerabilities to these harms, particularly in open societies that are increasingly dependent on these technologies. Third, the unrestricted warfare strategy is working. Revisionist authoritarian states are using these vulnerabilities and others to weaken liberal democracies. At a time when the relative power of antiliberal states is rising, it's crucial that we quickly ascertain how we can defend ourselves against constant harms, including the disabling of a computer-aided dispatch (CAD) systems, logic bombs within critical infrastructure, costly cybercrime and cyber espionage, the alteration of voting machine information, and COVID vaccine disinformation—while remaining true to the norms that define and sustain us.

This volume's authors provide innovative and timely advice on these challenges. Michael Morell, former deputy and acting director of the Central Intelligence Agency, begins our inquiry into intelligence ethics with an insider's perspective on the CIA's efforts to apply ethical standards befitting a liberal democracy to secretive work against illiberal adversaries. Cécile Fabre and Michael Skerker delve further into the applicable ethical frameworks; and pieces by David Luban, Anthony Pfaff, David Omand, and Mitt Regan apply these frameworks to interrogational torture, intelligence gathering via technical and human means, and covert action. Turning to grey zone ethics, Helen Frowe and Edward Barrett recommend ethical frameworks for responding to low-level lethal and sublethal harms; and Michael Gross, Tamar Meisels, George Lucas, Jens Ohlin, and Orde Kittrie use these general principles to assess the morality of using and/or responding to propaganda, hostages, cyberattacks, election fraud, and lawfare.

In addition to providing resources for teaching, we hope that this unique volume will inspire further attention to at least two issues relevant to policy makersand practitioners. First, a lively debate remains about the appropriate general ethical principles. Regarding spying, unthreatening liberal societies and their intelligence professionals might find the hypothetical consent justification rather unpersuasive.[4] However, rights-respecting societies who want to appraise their security through spying, but frown on necessary/lesser evil justifications for harm, might be hard-pressed to use a rights forfeiture framework to justify harmful activities designed to discern threats. While preventive war is morally fraught in practice, at least it assumes that active intentions to unjustly harm have already been established. On responses to sublethal grey zone attacks, although liberal societies increasingly eschew treating wrongdoers as means by punishing them for the purpose of deterring others, it might be all-things-considered justifiable in some situations. Perhaps the method of "reflective equilibrium," which balances general principles and particular judgments, can be leveraged to clarify the principles that pertain to particular espionage and grey zone cases.[5]

Second, intelligence and military operations are complicated by the fact that intelligence and grey zone actors and activities often overlap, as indicated by the earlier mention of cyber espionage. For example, intelligence assets can be used for collecting information or for limited lethal operations to weaken another state. And cyber operators from intelligence or defense communities can conduct espionage to determine a state's military capabilities and intentions, or to steal intellectual property. Ultimately these activities should be differentiated by their purposes: intelligence operations seek to obtain or protect facts about a society's capabilities and intentions, while grey zone operations seek to directly weaken another society's capabilities. Intelligence and military professionals must be taught to make these functional distinctions in order to apply the relevant ethical principles.

NOTES

1. For the purpose of this preface, "intelligence activities," "spying," and "espionage" includes counterintelligence.
2. For a full treatment of these three justifications, see Cécile Fabre, *Spying through a Glass Darkly: The Ethics of Espionage and Counter-Intelligence* (Oxford, 2022).
3. See Qiao Liang and Wang Xiangsui, *Unrestricted Warfare* (Beijing: PLA Literature and Arts Publishing House, 1999).
4. For a similar perspective, see the "revisionist" critique of the supposed moral equality of combatants in war.
5. John Rawls, *A Theory of Justice* (Harvard University Press, 1971).

JUSTICE AT THE MARGINS OF WAR

1 | An Interview with Mr. Michael Morell, Former Deputy and Acting Director of the Central Intelligence Agency
Conducted by Mitt Regan & Edward Barrett

Mitt Regan: Michael, it's a great privilege to have you here—someone with such a distinguished career in the intelligence community, someone who also (some of you may know) was in fact in charge of the presidential daily brief of intelligence matters and was with President Bush on 9/11.

Mike, let me start with a basic threshold question that some people asked me. Does it even make sense to talk about ethics in the context of intelligence activities? In your book on your career in the CIA, you describe the agency as an organization that conducts espionage as a business, stealing secrets around the globe. A former colleague in the UK, David Omand, who was head of GCHQ—the new UK signals intelligence agency—said that to overcome the determination of a person with a secret to keep can require the use of ethically questionable methods: intruding on personal communications, breaking into homes to plant bugs, hacking networks, persuading others to betray their oaths of loyalty to their state or inform other colleagues. But if this weren't done then real secrets of value to the nation would not be obtained. All this, of course, is done in pursuit of a mission of protecting the country. So it would seem pretty easy to simply adopt the philosophy that the ends justify the means. Now, I know you don't think that's the case, but why not?

Michael Morell: I think that everything you just said, Mitt, you could say about the military. You could say that about killing other human beings as part of a military operation. And yet we all know that there are ethics involved there; you guys know them better than I do. But there are also ethics involved in intelligence operations and intelligence analysis, and there needs to be. And the reason there needs to be is because we are representing the American people, we're representing the U.S. government, and we don't just take an oath to the Constitution; we actually think about furthering the values of the nation, whether that be freedom or democracy, or what have you. So I don't think it's possible to represent the nation, to do the nation's work, without upholding the values of the nation. Does imposing ethical limits get in the way of intelligence operations? Sure. But I don't think we could sustain intelligence operations, sustain intelligence capabilities, without living within our values, and I think that's why it's so important.

Mitt Regan: And how are those values actually operationalized with respect to intelligence operations and intelligence activity? That is, what kinds of limits, based on those values, does the agency and the intelligence community believe are important?

Michael Morell: It starts with the people we hire. In my last year, there were 180,000 applications for a thousand jobs, so we really get our choice of America's best and brightest. And part of that is not only choosing talented people, but people who have the right values; people who we believe that we can trust; and, therefore, people who the Congress can trust; and, by extension, the American people. So, it starts with who we hire—quite frankly the polygraph is pretty useful in identifying people who might not have those values. It continues on day one when you take the oath of office, which I used to give the new officers. But then I would talk about more than just defending the Constitution. I would talk about what our job is, which is collecting information that others are trying to keep secret from us and why that's important, and then analyzing that. And then I would talk about how we expect officers to behave and to conduct themselves. And then those same kinds of values and ethics and tenets were reinforced in the introductory courses. And then I'd say, most importantly, they get reinforced day-to-day on the job, in terms of what decisions are made and what decisions aren't made.

Let me give you an example. When I was Leon Panetta's deputy, Leon and I and another senior officer from the agency had a meeting with Susan Rice, who was then the Ambassador to the United Nations. And in this meeting, a senior officer at the agency intentionally said something to Ambassador Rice that wasn't accurate. And Leon didn't know it at the time, but on the way back in the car, the three of us were talking about it, and I pointed this out to the director in front of his officer. And he didn't say anything at the time, but we came back to the agency, and he asked both of us to come into his office. And we sat down around his table, and he said to this senior officer, "Is what Michael said in the car true, that you knew that what you said was not accurate?" This officer said, "Yes." And Leon said, "Alright, that is strike one, and this is not baseball; you have one more shot. And if you do this again, you're gone." That story spread like wildfire across the agency. And it's those kinds of actions and decisions that reinforce what you're told on day one in what you learn in these classes.

Mitt Regan: I know the intelligence community adopted a set of ethical principles, I believe under D&I director Clapper at the time. On an ongoing basis, what kinds of things does the agency do to make sure that its employees understand how to apply those—let's say on the operations side with trying to cultivate human intelligence, for instance? Or any other kind of activities that the agency might conduct? As we know, when the rubber meets the road in ethics is, in particular situations, when people often don't have someone over their shoulder, and they have to use judgment. Are there things on an ongoing basis that the agency tries to do to ensure that people do act according to those ethical principles?

Michael Morell: The first thing I'd say—and I think this is important—is the very act of recruiting another human being to spy for the United States, the very act of asking them to commit espionage against their own country, to violate the law of their own country, to violate their own principles and ethics as they relate to their own country, you would think that's a kind of ethically blurry space. But I think it's not, and I think it's not because the most important ethic we have is that the search for the truth is the most important thing we do. And we have adversaries who are developing capabilities and have intentions and plans that would harm the United States, and they're trying to keep that secret from us, and, in order to protect ourselves, we need to find out what those secrets are.

So, that imperative overcomes the very notion of taking advantage of another human being when you ask them and get them to say "yes" to spying for you. And you are taking advantage of their vulnerabilities. In fact, when you're interacting with these people, you're trying to identify their vulnerabilities. What's a vulnerability? Somebody needs money, somebody has significant debts, somebody wants their kids to go to college in the United States, it's a vulnerability. Somebody has a wife who has a health issue and needs medical care in the West, that's a vulnerability, right? And we take advantage of those. What I think is important, though, is that there's a limit to that. The limit to that is we only use positive inducements. We say, "We'll give you money if you work for us. We'll take care of your wife's healthcare if you work for us. We'll make sure your kids get into the right schools if you work for us. If you work for us for a certain period of time, you can come to the United States." We do not use negative inducements, we do not use coercion, we do not use blackmail. In the past, in the far past of the agency, we did. But we've grown a lot since then, in many, many ways—including ethically. So those are things that are off the table today.

And then there's a whole set of rules that are actually written down on paper about two things. First, who we pretend to be when we're first interacting with people, so what is our cover—are we a state department officer, are we a military officer. There are certain things that are written on a piece of paper that we are not allowed to pretend to be. Somebody serving in the Peace Corps, a journalist, a medical professional, somebody of religious order, because we think that's not the right thing to do and would put those people at risk. And then there are rules with regard to who we can recruit, so there are certain categories of people who we cannot go after for similar reasons, and those are all documented.

And then the last thing I'd say is that CIA operations officers are not out on the streets acting on their own; they're not out there making decisions on their own. I don't want to discourage anybody from someday being interested in being an operations officer, but before you have any interaction with somebody that you're interested in, there is a pretty bureaucratic process that you go through for putting together a plan for how you're going to meet this person, what your conversation is going to be, what are the different possible ways that conversation can go, and what are your responses to their responses, etc. All that must be approved by the station chief wherever you are serving. And then in most cases that comes back to Washington to be approved. And then when you're done, you must write up a report on exactly what happened, and you have to brief your chief of station on it. So, this is not folks out there acting on their own. There's very, very close supervision here because of the consequences of getting caught, because of the consequences of doing something wrong.

Mitt Regan: So, if we move to another area of activity, what's sometimes called political action, it's common knowledge that countries attempt to influence events in other countries. Sometimes that takes the form of providing assistance to groups that may oppose a regime. In the 1980s, for instance, assistance to Solidarity in Poland, and perhaps assistance to the Mujahideen in Afghanistan, assistance to the Contras in opposing Nicaraguan government. Some of those have been controversial, others less so. But what kinds of ethical principles should guide U.S. efforts to influence the political dynamics in other countries?

Michael Morell: I am so glad you asked this question. We are now talking about what you know to be covert action. And the question that you're asking is a policy question; it's not an intelligence question. The decision to undertake a covert action, to include the specific activities that the CIA will undertake on behalf of the United States, is a policy decision. That decision is made by the President in writing with the advice and counsel of his or her national security team—so it's a policy question about what the ethics of covert action are.

I think the interesting intelligence question is the way this works. The White House comes to the CIA, and it says, "I'm trying to achieve this policy objective, this particular policy objective. I'm trying to"—I'm going to make this up—"I'm trying to slow down the Iranian nuclear program. They're pursuing a nuclear weapon and I want to do anything I can to slow it down. What can you do for me?" And those ideas are often generated at the agency. Sometimes they're generated in policy circles, but they're often generated at the agency and they are brought back to the policy makers for discussion. So, the real intelligence question is, as a senior officer at CIA, do you take every legal option that you think would be effective back to the president, or do you only take the ones that you are morally comfortable with yourself? That is a really interesting question. Do you get to be the decider of the options that go in front of the president, or do you take all the options forward?

And I think different directors would answer that question differently. I know that Mike Hayden would say it's my responsibility to take to the president any option that is legal that I think would be effective. It's for the president to decide. My view is a little bit different. My view is that my morals and my ethics matter here. It's my organization; I'm in charge, I have to lead. I have to have the respect of my officers in order to lead. And so I'm going to make some decisions about what I take forward and what I don't. That's the interesting question.

And I would just finish up here: there's a tremendous amount of controversy about enhanced interrogation techniques done by the Bush administration in the immediate aftermath of 9/11. And I do a lot of talks like this around the country, and I always get asked about it. And to drive home the point that we've just talked about, that what you do in covert action is a policy decision and not an intelligence decision, I will always say, "Look, I will talk to you about this for as long as you want. We can go on for hours in talking about this in every detail, if you accept one proposition: if you accept the proposition that this was not the CIA's program. It was directed by the president, approved by his national security team, approved by the attorney general, multiple attorney generals on multiple occasions, and briefed to Congress with their support. So as long as we agree this is America's program and not CIA's, let's have a conversation about it."

Mitt Regan: Let me follow up on that. John Brennan's recent memoirs—he was deputy executive director at the agency at the time, and got information about the enhanced interrogation program from then-director George Tenet—basically said he was uneasy about it. And Tenet said, "Well, I want you to make sure that nothing's being done that hasn't been explicitly authorized by DOJ, Department of Justice." And Brennan said, "That's the problem, George. We're not doing anything in violation, but I still have some concerns." And he says in his book, I just wrote a short quote, "I've committed many sins of omission during my lifetime, but I consider my failure at the time to convey my concern about the program in clear and unequivocal terms to George and other senior members as my most egregious." In retrospect, do you think that those such as he, and perhaps others who had those kinds of concerns, should have been more forceful in raising them at the time?

Michael Morell: Absolutely, absolutely. In any profession, and in intelligence and military operations in particular, I think if you are uneasy morally about something that your organization is doing, that you have a responsibility to speak up. But I also want to add that the greatest responsibility is on the part of the leader in creating an environment where people feel comfortable raising issues like that. And George—I was George's executive assistant and I know him extraordinarily well—created that kind of atmosphere, created the kind of atmosphere where John felt comfortable coming into his office and saying that. Now John admits that he should have gone even further. And so an interesting question then would be, "What if John had said, 'I just can't abide by this. This, for me, is morally reprehensible'?" Then I think John's got to do what John thinks is right in terms of whether he can continue to serve in that position, whether he can continue to serve at the agency.

But I think the more interesting question is, "What's George's responsibility if a senior officer comes to him and expresses deep concern about this?" George would tell you that he had already had a conversation with a number of people about the morality of this, and they knew they were on shaky grounds—including with Condi Rice about the morality of this. But I do think that had John really expressed his concern, it would have been on George to share that concern with the White House: "I just want you to know that one of my most senior officers—in fact, one of the ones that I respect the most—is deeply uneasy about this, and I just need to share that with you." So I do think it's the responsibility of officers to speak up, I do think it's the responsibility of leaders to create the environment for them to speak up, but I think it's also the responsibility of leaders then to share that up the chain of command.

Mitt Regan: Then stepping back from that program with the benefit of some hindsight—it's obviously been a tremendous flash point for the agency—stepping back now, as you look at it, are there lessons learned from that program that are valuable for the agency and the intelligence community in going forward?

Michael Morell: Absolutely, absolutely. There are many, many, many lessons. The first one, and maybe the most important one, is when we were approached and asked to be the nation's jailers of terrorists, we should have said, "No. We're not in that business." This was a decision that Secretary Rumsfeld made. He didn't want to be in that business. Eventually he got into that business at Guantanamo and some other places, but he didn't want to be. We should have said no. And when we were asked to do interrogations, we should have said, "No, we don't know anything about that. We're not trained interrogators." When we started this, we had no idea what we were doing, literally no idea what we were doing, from the concept of running a prison to the concept of conducting interrogations: no idea, no training, no background, no experience, no history.

Look, one of the mistakes that I've seen made over and over and over again by CIA is that it's too quick to say yes to covert action. Presidents turn too quickly to CIA for help when they have a really sticky foreign policy problem, and the agency is too quick to say yes—simply because it wants to be helpful, it wants to help the president achieve his or her objectives. But I think the agency really needs to think about whether what it can do can really be effective in moving the policy needle, and whether what it's being asked to do will have long-term impact on the agency in terms of its capabilities and in terms of its reputation. I tried. When I was acting director, there were a couple of requests from the Obama administration for us to think about covert action with regard to areas where we had never done it before, and my answer to Denis McDonough and Tom Donilon was, "We can't help you. We could put together a program that costs $200 million and we could do a bunch of stuff, but it's not going to move the policy needle for you; it's just not. It's going to make you feel good, but it's not going to move the needle. So, no, we don't think this a good idea."

Mitt Regan: One of the concepts that's arisen from that and become more popular in recent years in thinking about the military ethics and particularly those who are serving in combat, is this concept of moral injury. Which is just the sense, I'll paraphrase it, of disillusionment in the value of any kind of moral principles at all. Some of the figures in some of the John le Carré novels might be said to be suffering from moral injury. Is that a risk given the kind of work that the agency does? And to the extent it is, does the agency try to be alert to that and take steps to try to intervene?

Michael Morell: That's a great question. So here you have, in this intelligence business, you have intelligence officers who are authorized to break the laws of other countries. Not our own laws, mind you, but the laws of other countries. What impact does that have on them and their willingness to write in their own morality, and their willingness to act in accordance with the standards that we set? Look, we have our share of operations officers who get themselves into trouble in a variety of different ways, like many organizations. But it is interesting to me that—and we never did a study on this, probably should have—it's interesting that operations officers seem to get themselves into more trouble than other officers at the agency—analysts, support officers, scientists, and engineers, etc. In fact, I'd say for a group of people that account for maybe 20 percent of the organization, they seem to have 80 percent of the problems. So maybe this is exactly what you're talking about.

We had programs in place to make it difficult for people to do the wrong thing. When you pay an asset, when you pay a spy money, you actually get them to sign a receipt. Why? To make sure that the operations officer isn't paying the asset less than the organization thinks it's paying and pocketing the rest. That's why you do it. So there are all these auditing trails and all sorts of things that any compliance officer in any large organization would recognize. But do we pay attention to this from a psychological perspective and look out for it from a human resources care perspective? No. But your question suggests to me that we should.

Mitt Regan: Interesting. But it's not hard to imagine why those in operations might be particularly prone to that. You spent most of your career on the analysis side. In what ways could that arise for analysts, as well as those in operations?

Michael Morell: The sin on the analytics side of the agency is something we call politicization, which is somebody in the process—from the analyst all the way to the final consumer—changing the analysis in a way that is inconsistent with what the analysts really think. And it can happen in any part of that process, including the analysts themselves. The risk the analysts themselves face is twofold. One is we're supposed to do analysis that is objective and is in no way impacted by politics or policy preferences. And so, you're not supposed to think about what you think the right thing to do on a particular policy issue is if you're the analyst. But if you are an analyst working on Afghanistan right now, you can't help but have a policy view about what the right thing to do is. So you have to work very hard yourself, and your managers have to work very hard with you, to make sure that your view of what the president should do about Afghanistan doesn't affect your analysis of the situation. So that's one way that analysts themselves can politicize, if they let their policy views impact their analysis.

The other thing that analysts have to be careful of is not wanting to please somebody in a chain of command above them, and having an analyst think that "I know what my boss wants to hear," or, "I know what the director wants to hear," or, "I know what the secretary of state wants to hear," or, "I know what the president wants to hear." And, therefore, you tilt your analysis in that direction. That's the analyst also politicizing intelligence analysis. Those are the two ways that analysts can mess up with regard to this extraordinarily important ethic in our business. There's a tremendous amount of training around this, there's a tremendous amount of conversation around it. There's an ombudsman that people can go to and say, "Hey, I think there's something funny here going on with the analysis," and the ombudsman can look into it. So, are we perfect? No. But I think we try very, very, very hard to make sure that that analysis is based on the facts and is objective in terms of being independent from politics and policy preferences.

Mitt Regan: I want to talk for a moment about something that might seem antithetical to intelligence activities, and that is transparency. When Stella Rimington took over as the director, MI5, the British domestic security and intelligence agency, she spearheaded initiatives to try to explain more to the public what MI5 was doing. Mark Pythian—who has co-written a book with David Omand, formerly of GCHQ—has said that secrecy is obviously essential in the intelligence community [IC], but it also creates a distance between the IC and citizens, which can then foster, perhaps, all sorts of ideas that the IC is part of the deep state, or the IC is doing a whole range of things that are problematic. Do you think that it is important for the IC to be more sensitive to that? And if so, what steps could be taken in the direction of transparency while still protecting sources and methods?

Michael Morell: Obviously sources and methods have to be protected, because if you don't protect them, then you lose the ability to collect, so obviously they have to be protected. Having said that, the problem that you raise is real. There has to be a way in a democratic society to give the American public a sense that the secret organizations who are operating in a democracy are doing the job that they're supposed to be doing, are using the taxpayers' money wisely, and are acting consistent with the Constitution, with domestic law, and with our values. And how do you do that?

Well, one of the ways you do that is through the system that we've created in Congress with these oversight committees. But I'll be very honest with you: the oversight committees don't really do their job with regard to that. They're not out talking to the American people about what we're doing in those three areas I talked about. They're focused on other things—we can talk more about that if you want. But they're essentially not doing that job. Whereas that's exactly what they're supposed to be doing on behalf of their colleagues in Congress and on behalf of the American people.

So, I do think it does fall back on the leadership of the intelligence community to be as transparent as you can possibly be. And my own personal view is that we could be a lot more transparent. I think there is plenty of room to push out the fence line in terms of what we can talk about. And by pushing it out—and explaining what we do and why we do it and how well we do it and talking about general successes and general failures—I think you can actually help educate the American people, make them feel more comfortable about these secret organizations and how they're operating. And I think you can actually, in the process, do a better job of protecting the secrets you have to protect.

Mitt Regan: Any example of a way?

Michael Morell: I think the senior leadership has to get out a lot, a lot. This has never been done to the level that I think it needs to be done. And in the Trump administration, the senior leadership in the IC went dark, they didn't want to speak in public at all because they didn't want to upset their boss. I think Gina Haspel, in her three years as director, had two public appearances. Two in three years. It should be one a week—colleges, universities, think-tanks, world affairs councils, civic groups. So, I think the leadership has to be out there and be seen. I think the leadership has to be open to talking to the media more than they do. There's something that Leon did that I thought was extraordinarily helpful, which was we would, once every two weeks or so, he and I would have an off-the-record dinner in his dining room at the agency with six or seven reporters. And we wouldn't tell them secrets, but we would show a lot of leg, and it was an attempt to give them more insight into what we were doing so that the American people had a better understanding. I thought that was very important.

Then the last thing I'll say is: the declassification process. We're behind. We're woefully behind. We need to do a better job on that. And it's certainly important to put the documents out so that academics and reporters can go through them, but I'd like to find a way to bring into popular culture the declassified stories of the past. In fact, what I'm thinking of suggesting is instead of putting out a five-hundred-page study—when you declassify a whole bunch of documents, you have one of your historians put out a five-hundred-page study that very few people are going to read—make a documentary and put it on YouTube. Just make sure it's accurate, no spinning; you have to do successes and failures. But make the history more accessible to the American people than it's made today.

Mitt Regan: Well, Michael, I could happily continue this conversation for the rest of the afternoon, but I won't. I want to close our segment by thanking you for your candor and your insight, and I'm going to turn it over now to Ed Barrett, whom I think has been fielding questions from folks. So, thank you so much again. It's a real pleasure to see you again.

Michael Morell: Good to see you.

Ed Barrett: Thanks very much, Mitt. I have some really good questions from the midshipmen. The first asks about situations where you're gathering information from groups that don't have the same standards as we do. And he asks, "How do you fight the urge to cut those corners given the high stakes of the mission?"

Michael Morell: Well, you don't. You don't. You simply don't. The second half of my career was dominated with terrorism and counterterrorism. I'd say six out of every sixteen hours a day that I worked was probably counterterrorism. It was the plurality of what I did with my time. And it's very easy to think that they should be treated in a different way than, say, people who work for a nation-state. But you have to fight that urge.

I'll give you two examples. People often ask me about the mood in the room when Bin Laden was killed. And what I tell them, which is the truth, is that it was not like a locker room. There wasn't a lot of cheering and high-fiving and anything like that. Why? Because we had just killed several human beings—terrorists for sure—several human beings, we had killed a couple of civilians, killed one of the wives, and we had scared the wits out of a whole bunch of children. It's hard to overstate how hysterical these kids were in that compound. And when you think about that, all of a sudden, it takes away the urge to have that locker room atmosphere.

The other thing I'd say is that sometimes operations would end in my office, either as deputy director or acting director, when somebody would come in my office and say, "Hey, we'd like to do this. We need your approval." And it just didn't feel right to me from a moral perspective, and I would say, "No, I don't like this. Find another way. I know you guys are good enough to find another way." And oftentimes in counterterrorism, it was who we were willing to use as assets to get close to them. And we actually made some mistakes in that regard; I wish I could talk about them, but we made some mistakes in that regard, Leon and I. By the way, when folks would come in my office and run an operation by me, the ethical test that I would give it was, if this became public, would I be proud, would I be proud that my agency did this? Or would I not be proud, would I want to hide? And that was my moral compass that I operated by; it was taking my internal moral compass and applying it to the situation at hand. A lot of those were on counterterrorism, and I think there was a sense below me that maybe we can cut some corners, but I think it's extraordinarily important not to—because you start cutting corners in one place, you're not going to stop.

Ed Barrett: In those types of situations—and this involves another question—where a policy maker, for example, might be asking you to cut corners and do something unlawful or unethical or both, how are CIA officers instructed to deal with those situations?

Michael Morell: So, unlawful is different than unethical. If somebody asks you to do something unlawful, you say no. If you're aware of something unlawful being done, your responsibility is to go to the FBI or the Department of Justice. I'm not joking. If it's unethical, then we're back to the John Brennan situation, where your responsibility is to speak up. But when it comes to, say, covert action, it's the president's call again. So the president can say, "Thanks for your view but I want you to do this. I don't think it's unethical, go ahead." Then you have to make a decision about whether you want to continue to work there, whether you're the director or anybody else.

Ed Barrett: Our next question involves the effect of eliminating the Enhanced Interrogation Techniques program. His question is, "Do you believe that the new policies regarding ethical and moral limits on decisions made on the various levels of intelligence collections are a direct result of these changes?" And I think you addressed that somewhat before, concerning the effect of this program on the overall moral climate at the CIA.

Michael Morell: I think at the end of the day, one of the consequences of Enhanced Interrogation Techniques was that it gave the CIA—remember I talked earlier about how the CIA needs to stand up more to policy makers in saying no—I think Enhanced Interrogation Techniques steeled the spine of many CIA officers in saying no. In saying no to a White House that might want to do something that while lawful—and in this case, it's questionable whether they were actually lawful at the end of the day, so the DOJ had its own set of issues with regard to this. But I think it's steeled the spine, certainly steeled the spine in me.

Ed Barrett: Another question, a good one from a midshipman. You said that part of the ethic of an intelligence analyst is ensuring that policy or political preferences do not impact analysis. If the CIA itself is politicized by elected officials, does that make it more difficult for analysts to achieve this impartiality, and if so, what can be done to mitigate this problem?

Michael Morell: There are two separate issues. Great question, two separate issues. One is the policy maker putting pressure on the organization to see something a certain way. In the Bush administration, this was Scooter Libby putting intense pressure on CIA to come to the judgment that there was a relationship between Iraq and Al-Qaeda when we didn't think there was, and we didn't bend in that case. You have to stand up to the policy maker in saying, "No, that's not the way we see it. This is the way we see it, whether you like it or not." The other is when a senior official, policy official, goes out publicly and says, "This is what the intelligence community thinks," when it's not what we think. That happens. In that case, I think it's the responsibility of the leadership of the IC to go to that person and say, "You got this wrong. We did not say this. That's not what we think." And if it continues, to go to the boss of that person and have a conversation with that boss. So those are the two areas where senior policy makers can get involved in politization, and the intelligence community has a responsibility to respond in both of them.

Ed Barrett: Thank you. Let me pose at least one more question. What do you think about increased paramilitary operations in the CIA? Are these operations more morally problematic if not done by conventional military?

Michael Morell: Yeah, great question. Okay, so I can't talk about what the CIA does or doesn't do. But I will tell you this, I am an extraordinarily strong believer that our nation's military should do military operations, and that CIA should not. And it's not a moral issue for me. It's an issue of sucking the resources of CIA away from its fundamental mission of collecting and analyzing intelligence to do something that the military is much better capable of doing. When you have these paramilitary programs at CIA, Congress gives you money for them, but they don't give you more people. So, it sucks people away from the main mission, it takes your best people because this stuff is interesting and sexy, and it takes the time of the senior leadership because you don't want to get anything wrong because it's so edgy. You're probably all thinking about a program that I'm thinking of. I would have moved that from CIA a long, long time ago. So I couldn't agree more with the idea. Let me also put it this way, and I'm not admitting anything by saying this: I don't think the nation's civilian intelligence agency should be in the business of killing anybody.

Ed Barrett: Okay, this is a good capstone question. What are the greatest ethical challenges facing the intelligence community in the coming decades as our military strategy shifts to a more traditional great power competition with rising adversaries, especially China?

Michael Morell: Yeah, so I don't know if this is an ethical issue. It's just the issue. Intelligence faces an existential threat—literally, an existential threat—from ubiquitous persistent surveillance. The ability to conduct espionage, the ability to conduct human operations in a place where there are cameras recording everything 24/7, doing facial recognition, doing biometrics, etc., etc., is impossible. A lot of people don't know this, but a good chunk of our SIGINT is human-enabled; we recruit a human asset that gets us into a place to collect signals intelligence. So without these humans, not only is

CIA in trouble, but so is NSA. And quite frankly NSA faces its own problems from 5G and other challenges. So how the intelligence community responds to this technology challenge is going to determine whether they stay relevant or not in the future.

2 | The Ethics of Espionage
Cécile Fabre

I will start with some fairly broad setting-the-stage remarks on the ethics of espionage and counterintelligence, before setting my own views.

The first thing to note is that the ethics of espionage is a neglected question in just war theory and applied ethics more widely. I find this utterly mystifying. Espionage and counterintelligence, after all, are an important part of warfare. One would expect that philosophy, which has something to say about pretty much anything under the sun in general and about war in particular, would have something to say about espionage and its counterpart counterintelligence. I don't really have a good explanation for such neglect. In any event, I decided a few years ago to write a book on this. Like most people, I love espionage in its fictional and empirical nonfictional form. This is, I think, the only research project I've ever conducted where I can combine my love for philosophy with my love for that kind of stuff.

More importantly, however, espionage raises deeply interesting philosophical questions. Espionage and counterintelligence operations are activities which states conduct at our behest and on our behalf, and during which, they inflict a wide range of harms on people who are spied upon. Like any activity of that kind, it does stand in need of moral justification.

Moreover, espionage also connects in interesting ways to other areas of philosophy, foremost among which is the topic of decision-making under conditions of uncertainty. This topic has received quite a bit of attention recently at the hands of Anglo American political and moral philosophers. It addresses the following question: Supposing that I do not know what the facts of the matter are, what am I morally permitted to do?

The question of espionage is somewhat different. It asks the following: what am I morally permitted, or indeed morally obliged, to do to reduce the level of uncertainty under which I operate? These are not the same questions. But they are related, of course, in the following way.

Suppose that I do not know whether the facts are such that I am, as a military commander, morally permitted to issue an order to bomb a particular target. For example, I do not know whether this target is a military target or a civilian building. The first question asks, "What I'm morally permitted to do given that I do not know what this site is?" The second question asks, "What am I morally permitted to do as a commander in order to find out whether the target is a legitimate target?" Now, suppose next that I think, but do not know for sure, that a particular piece of information would enable me to find out whether the target is a military target, and therefore a legitimate target. I cannot procure this piece of information unless I spy on some people. So, we can ask again, "Given that I do not know whether having this piece of information will help me, what am I morally permitted to do under conditions of uncertainty?"

This is how I frame the question of espionage. It has to do with the acquisition of sensitive information, which (as far as we know) the other side does not really want us to have, and which we need to conduct our foreign policy. I frame the question of counterintelligence as what it is that we are morally entitled or obliged to do in order to protect information which we do not want the other side to have—again in the context of foreign policy writ large.

As I noted earlier, there is very little philosophical literature on the ethics of espionage (by which I mean, as a shortcut, espionage and counterintelligence in the remainder of my remarks). However, "very little" does not mean "none at all." We can distinguish broadly between three different approaches, in the scant literature there is. The first approach is the dirty-hands approach. It goes something like this: states need information about the other side to decide how to conduct their foreign policy. The means which they must employ to get that information are dirty means, such as deception, manipulation, exploitation, blackmail, and so on. States and their intelligence officials are morally entitled to resort to those means, thereby dirtying their hands.

I do not find this approach very convincing. It says that using those methods is morally wrong, although not as wrong as not using them in the first instance. I want to say, and I try to argue in my book, that sometimes using those methods is in fact morally right: one does not dirty one's hands in so doing.

The second approach relies on the social contract. It is the one developed by Michael Skerker, and he will describe it in detail in his own contribution. Let me outline here my objection to it. The social contract approach appeals to two important values, or norms: the norm of reciprocity on the one hand, and respect for rights on the other hand. At the bar of reciprocity, it says, "Well, look, we have a practice, which is the practice of intelligence protection and acquisition. So long as it doesn't violate some *malum in se* norms such as interrogational torture, we must accept that it is reasonable that we all engage in its constituent activities. If I send my spies to investigate what goes on in your embassy, you can't complain. If you send your spies to investigate what goes on in my embassies, I can't complain. I would like to do the same." At the bar of respect for rights, it says, "the aim of this approach is to ensure, as much as we can, that individuals' fundamental rights are respected."

However, it is not entirely clear to me how those two norms relate to each other. In particular, does it matter at all whether intelligence activities are carried out in defense of individual rights? If so, then it would seem that when acting reciprocally does not enable us to respect rights, we ought not so to act. So, reciprocity is merely instrumental; yet the social contract approach tends to treat it as fundamental. I know that contractarian approaches to war, particularly recent such approaches, have tried to square this particular circle, but I'm not entirely sure that they have succeeded in doing so.

The third approach, as you might have expected, draws on just war theory. It says that in the same way as we ought to distinguish the question of the moral norms that should govern the resort to war from the question of the moral norms that ought to regulate conduct in war, we should do the same with espionage. So for example, in the same way as war is morally permissible or just only if it has a just cause, espionage is morally permissible only if it has a just cause; in just the same way as war is morally permissible only if it is a proportionate response to the attack to which we are subjected, espionage is morally permissible only if it is a proportionate means of obtaining the information that we need.

I worry, however, that we run the risk of applying to the question of espionage and counterintelligence the very same principles that govern the resort to conduct in war in too mechanistic a fashion. The difficulty is that, to point out the obvious, to go to war is to kill; but to spy is not the same as to kill. To be sure, the means which intelligence agencies employ to procure the information needed by their pay masters or to protect information about us are harmful means. They consist in, for example, invasions of privacy, in blackmail, exploitation, manipulation, and so forth. So, although it is, I believe, appropriate to employ or to develop principles for the morally permissible imposition of harm, when you think of espionage, we must never lose sight of the fact that, to repeat, to spy is not the same as to kill.

None of these three approaches are fully satisfactory. What then is my own view? In my book I argue that espionage and counterintelligence are morally justified only in pursuit of morally justified ends. Indeed, on some views, the moral status of the ends is irrelevant. In contrast, my approach uses the language of rights forfeiture. I argue that citizens and their political communities have a pro tanto right that important information about themselves should remain secret. Under some circumstances, however, they can be deemed to have forfeited the right to secrecy such that the victims of the unjust foreign policy which their community conduct, or parties which act on behalf of these victims, acquire the right to procure those secrets. To put the point differently, if citizens and officials of a particular political community give us good reason to believe that they are derelict in their duty not to cause us wrongful harm, we have a probable cause to investigate further by means of espionage. The same point applies if we have reason to believe that they are derelict in their duty not to cause wrongful harm to third parties. In other words, we are morally permitted (and in fact sometimes are under a duty) to carry out those activities not just for our sake (in the context of, e.g., national self-defense) but also for the same of strangers (in the context of, e.g., a humanitarian intervention). This framework makes intuitive sense to me: It's a good way of understanding why there are morally important differences between citizens and their political communities, and the intelligence agencies which act on their behalf, depending on the moral status of the foreign policy ends which they pursue.

This leads me to make some controversial claims in the book, and I will highlight four. First, some of the means which intelligence agencies use to procure information or secrets about the other side and to defend their own are morally justified. These are means which normally would elicit very strong moral criticisms. To give you an example, as you may know, Immanuel Kant strongly objected to espionage. He called it, in a fit of particular vituperative denunciation, that "infernal art." The reason why Kant strongly objected to espionage is because espionage, he thought, necessarily involves deception. As you know, Kant had very strong objections to deception in general, and to lying in particular. Yet, as I argue in the book, under some conditions, deception via intelligence agencies in the service of morally justified ends is morally the right thing to do. In fact, our intelligence agencies are sometimes morally obliged to resort to it.

Second, espionage raises the difficult issue of treason. More often than not, the human agents thanks to whom we acquire information about our enemies are themselves members of the other side. They are, in effect, betraying their own side for the sake of helping us. At least, this is how they would be regarded if they were found out by their fellow citizens and leaders. It seems to me therefore that an ethics of espionage and counterintelligence must look at the morality of treason. I argue that under some conditions, not only is it morally permissible to betray one's country for the sake of just ends, it is in fact, morally speaking, the required thing to do.

Third, I also argue that, under some circumstances, we are morally permitted to spy on our allies—particularly when the alliance is clearly one of pure geostrategic expediency and when we have reasons to believe that our "ally" will betray us at the first opportunity. Espionage between the United States and UK on the one hand and the USSR on the other hand during World War II (from 1941 onward) comes to mind here.

Finally, I argue that economic espionage is morally justified in the service of just ends framed by reference to national security broadly construed. I mention this claim here because economic espionage has received even less attention than espionage tout court, including in the empirical literature. It seems to me that a robust defense of espionage in general yields the conclusion that economic espionage under some circumstances is morally justified. By economic espionage, I mean, the practice by which states and their intelligence agencies collect economic information about private economic corporations. My claim is that the economic nature of the information thereby acquired and the nature of the agents from which it is acquired does not in itself license us to condemn those practices as morally objectionable. Again, the moral status of the ends which we thereby pursue makes a crucial difference. The underlying thought is this: If you think that espionage in the service of national security is morally permissible pro tanto; if you think that the national security ought to be constructed not just in narrow military terms, but in wider terms, so as to include the critical infrastructure of our country; and if you also think that it is morally permissible that private economic actors should play as important a part as they do currently in maintaining and sustaining some of that critical infrastructure, then I think it becomes extremely difficult, not to say impossible, to draw in a sharp line between the political-military on the one hand, and the economic on the other hand.

The book is not meant to be exhaustive. It focuses on espionage and counterintelligence as collecting and protecting information. It does not consider other activities which some intelligence agencies carry out, such as covert, paramilitary operations. Of the many other issues it does not address, one warrants mentioning here, namely whether asymmetrical conflicts, between militarily weak and militarily strong actors, ought to be governed by different espionage norms. For example, we might think that sexual blackmail is not a morally permitted way of getting information about the enemy. But suppose that a military weak actor has no other means to do so. Suppose further that its cause is just. Should we relax the norm as far as it is concerned, but maintain it as far as the strong actor is concerned? Or suppose that the only way to eradicate a transnational terrorist network, whose members show complete disregard for the rights of others, is by resorting to means usually regarded as impermissible. Does the nature of our enemy imply that we can relax those rules? Similar issues arise with the ethics of warfare itself. I am tempted to answer in the negative in both cases. But more work needs to be done here.

I do not know, to conclude, why it is that philosophers have up until now neglected the ethics of espionage. It is a fascinating topic in and of itself, but also, to reiterate, it enables us to think about much broader and much deeper questions in moral and political philosophy—questions which behooves us not just as scholars, but as citizens as well, to address.

3 | A Contractualist Framework for Intelligence Ethics
Michael Skerker

I'm going to present my theory of intelligence operations with a focus on SIGINT and IMINT. The first part of the theory relies on foundational work done by Seumas Miller. Human beings have natural human rights and, when they live in groups, joint moral rights. Those are rights that attach to individuals, but only as members of groups, like the right to secede, the right to cultural determination, and most importantly, for our purposes, the right to collective security. The aggregation of individual and joint moral rights, as well as the needs for certain basic collective goods for a flourishing life, create collective moral responsibilities for groups to deliver these goods and protect these rights, because only groups have the ability to efficiently, effectively, and expertly deliver these goods and respect these rights on a wide scale.

For example, only large-scale social cooperation can create a secure environment, clean air and water, a robust healthcare system, infrastructure, and so on. So, people have individual duties to others that are active in a one-on-one basis. They also have collective moral responsibilities to contribute to their common good. Now, like joint moral rights, these collective moral responsibilities attach to individuals, but only when they're parts of certain groups. Typically, for laypeople, those outside certain vital professions, the collective moral responsibility is executed by supporting or creating institutions to address those relevant rights, like schools, hospitals, governments, churches, militaries, and intelligence agencies. Once just institutions exist, the collective moral responsibility to protect others' rights and deliver certain goods is largely acquitted by supporting these institutions. Support can be done by paying tax, by not actively trying to subvert these institutions, by volunteering on their behalf, and importantly, by cooperating with professionals who work for these institutions.

So, laypeople have a moral duty to support just institutions, in short, because they have a duty to protect the rights of other people or respect the rights of other people, and these institutions allow them to respect the rights of millions of people. Now, the professionals who work in these vital institutions can acquit their collective moral responsibilities by working diligently in their professions, by adhering to properly constituted professional norms. Since these institutions are created to acquit collective moral responsibilities, professionals in these institutions have a moral duty to comply with their properly constituted professional imperatives. Now, what this means is that it's not just a fiduciary obligation to do their job well because they are getting paid, but there is a moral duty if they are in these professions to adhere to properly constituted professional norms.

It is through those norms that one can respect others' rights and deliver certain morally essential goods. From this point on, I will be departing from Seumas Miller's work. Properly constituted professional norms guide professionals to do three things. They serve their clients' needs; respect the rights of non-clients; and, also, uphold their—the professionals'—own rights and dignity. So, if we're talking about the sphere of intelligence ethics, like all professional ethics, intelligence ethics involves the balancing of the rights and interests of three stake-holding groups: the professionals themselves, their clients and all non-clients, and especially their targets. So, in a sense, we can ask three times from the perspective of each of these groups, what is reasonable to demand of the other two groups. In the abstract, we can see that these groups ought to all endorse norms and tactics that strike an optimal balance between being practically efficacious on one hand, and rights-respecting on the other hand. This is because everybody wants physical security and at a low cost in terms of infringements on their rights. Infringements on their rights include infringements when they are the beneficiaries of the security-seeking tactics and especially when they are the targets of these security-seeking operations.

I conceive of tactics as specific applications of general norms. For example, if police have the norm that we ought to treat people as innocent until proven guilty, that will lead to specific tactics like getting warrants before searching domiciles or advising suspects of their rights when they are arrested. I mentioned before "properly constituted professional norms." On my view, professional norms can be identified with what I call the security standard. This is a hypothetical consensual model that does three things. First, it canvasses technologically and economically feasible options for a given intelligence agency. Second, it isolates those norms and tactics that work the best, which is to say, the most reliable, efficacious, proportionate, and efficient tactics of those that are locally feasible. And third, and most importantly, it endorses those that are the most rights-respecting among the tactics that meet the practical norms, the practical standards in number two. Now, for those of you who follow this debate in the social contract literature, I am not saying that hypothetical consent makes these norms binding on professionals. Rather, I'm saying this security standard merely identifies the proper content of intelligence norms. It is the collective moral responsibility to deliver security that grounds the norms and makes them morally binding on intelligence professionals.

The idea is that intelligence officers have a collective moral responsibility to help deliver security to their countries. It's the security standard that identifies the proper norms they ought to obey while they're executing that collective moral responsibility. We have three stakeholder groups whose rights we need to respect. The rights of clients of intelligence officers are largely met by selecting the most practically efficacious tactics, the ones that actually work to lead to national security. Intelligence officers are not doing their job if they pick shoddy techniques. Now, certain efficacious norms or tactics might have to be excluded because of the moral, psychological, or physical damage done to the operators themselves, particularly in the human intelligence context. This might, for example, preclude interrogatory torture, or the use of sexual seduction in the cultivation of sources. We know these kinds of things lead to the moral and psychological injury of the agents who perpetrate them. The rights of intelligence targets will also eliminate some practically efficacious options.

Yet what's complex about this is that not all intelligence targets will have the same bevy of rights. We need to talk about how certain targets can lose or give up certain baskets of rights. And I think there are three general relevant ways to give up or have a right taken away from you. The first two are no doubt familiar. You can forfeit a right by violating someone else's right or threatening to violate someone else's right. The rights violator forfeits certain rights that are necessary for the defender or a proxy to infringe upon in the course of a proportionate defense. And the relevant intelligence targets who perhaps forfeit a right to privacy are members of unprivileged irregular militant groups like Al-Qaeda, Al-Shabaab, Boko Haram, ISIS, pirates, international drug dealers—criminals of that sort. They give up a right to privacy, especially regarding their tactical secrets, their work product, because their tactical secrets concern plots that are meant to violate other people's rights. They can't insist on a right to keep those things secret. A waiver is a consensual giving up of certain rights to certain people for certain periods of time and certain purposes. The paradigmatic example is a rugby player waiving his right to other rugby players to be tackled in certain ways for the duration of the game. I agree with other scholars, like Tony Pfaff, who argue that intelligence officers waive their rights to privacy when they enter the intelligence sphere voluntarily. They know they're entering a domain where they will be asked to collect intelligence on their foreign counterparts and they will be subject to intelligence collection in turn because they are handling security-sensitive information. Moreover, they are amply trained and equipped with tactics and gadgets meant to protect the privacy, particularly of their work product. In short, they know what they're getting into.

Finally, and perhaps the most complex, we concede rights as part of fulfilling a duty. If I have a duty to give you something like a tool that I borrowed from you, that means I've ceded a right to that tool. I can't keep it; I can't fight you if you come to collect it; I can't ask my friends to help me keep it; I can't sue you to retain it. I have to give it up when you want it back. Now, we've talked before about how we can respect the rights of many other people by supporting just institutions; we have a duty in fact to support just institutions. As part of that duty, I think, we cede claim-rights to the professionals in those institutions to engage in their security standard compliant protocols. For example, if I own a restaurant, I have the claim-right normally to kick out trespassers in my kitchen, but I must support a just public health department as a way of respecting the rights of diners in my restaurant and other people. So I cede claim-rights to public health inspectors who come asking to search my kitchen. I must cooperate with them; I can't get in their way; and so on. This is a way of respecting the rights of diners. As another example, I cede claim-rights to local police in my basically just state. If they want to search my home or arrest me with a warrant, it would be wrong for me to try and stop them. Again, my neighbors need to have competent just police to investigate and to deter crimes in order to respect their rights. So, to support the rights of my neighbors, I should permit competent police to investigate me if evidence suggests that I have committed a crime.

Now, that might not be so controversial, but I want to suggest that we also have duties to support just foreign institutions. People overseas need police, military, and intelligence protection, just as much as we do here in the United States. So, let's say, for example, if I am overseas in Oxford, England, attending a conference and I witness a mugging, I am morally obliged, I argue, to cooperate with British police as a way of supporting the rights of British subjects. It would be wrong for me to refuse and place a roadblock in their investigations. Let's talk about what kind of roadblocks one might put up in an intelligence context. To answer that we have to consider what a foreign intelligence agency might need from me. I'm a civilian ethics professor. Well, a foreign intelligence agency needs to confirm that I am just a civilian ethics professor, not an undercover intelligence operative, not a terrorist, not an international drug dealer who just chooses to drive a 2015 Toyota Camry. They need, in short, to discern if I am a threat. They need, I think, to engage in what I call diagnostic collection, some kind of light touch intelligence collection, just to see if I am a threat or if I'm in contact with known threats.

Now, this is a major difference between just intelligence theory and just war theory. It may signal a difference between Professor Fabre's approach and my own. Intelligence by its very nature has to be prophylactic, forward-leaning, horizon scanning. Intelligence officers can't limit their actions to known security threats because they need to scan the horizon and figure out where the next security threat exists. Therefore, they have to be able, I think, to engage in some kind of diagnostic collection prior to having the equivalent of probable cause in the law enforcement agency realm or just cause in the military realm. Let's say I agree in abstract that intelligence agencies have to engage in diagnostic collection in order to assess what threats exist. This is something the inhabitants of all states can and should demand of their intelligence agencies, and therefore it would be wrong for me to place a moral roadblock in the way of a foreign intelligence agency that is engaged in that morally upright action of trying to protect their citizens.

So the upshot is this: I think the duty to support just foreign institutions means that I must cede claim-rights against being diagnostically collected against so long as those foreign agents are adhering to security standard compliant protocols. Perhaps somewhat controversially, this pertains to foreign intelligence agencies who are engaged in the basic job of protecting their citizens against foreign military attacks, against terrorism, against piracy, against drug dealing, and so could cover the actions of agencies in various illiberal and even nefarious regimes. The idea is that inhabitants of oppressive or illiberal states still have a human right against being attacked by outside actors, be they service members or terrorists or pirates. It follows that a given agency might have moral permission to engage in diagnostic operations while also lacking permission to do illiberal things like spy on local peaceful dissidents.

What I have in mind about diagnostic operations will vary given technology, but could include, for example, metadata analysis or electronically scanning huge tranches of electronic data, looking for keywords. These are all meant to assess where the threats are. They're meant to identify as of yet unidentified threats. Now, in contrast to these automated computerized searches, where no human sees the content of messages, consider sustained collection targeted at specific people where the content is read by human analysts, or what I call collateral collection, where an innocent person's correspondence with an intelligence target is captured. These actions require forfeiture or waiver.

We've talked about how intelligence officers waive rights to privacy. I think that ordinary citizens can be modeled as waiving claim rights against more invasive collection, beyond diagnostic collection, if they can be modeled as endorsing the same sort of collection by their agencies. Let me say more about that. We can model that endorsement, given the security needs of the given country. Now as an analogy, I waive my rights against being countersued if I hire a lawyer to sue my neighbor. I can't begrudge him for hiring a lawyer to protect his interests and maybe countersuing me if I'm doing the very same thing. This idea suggests a reciprocal rule of intelligence collection. Any set of norms or tactics that I can reasonably demand of my intelligence agencies in order to keep me safe creates a standard for what inhabitants and adversary states can, in turn, demand of their agencies.

This collection might cover collateral collection, or targeted collection against individuals who are not members of the security establishment, for example, civilian scientists working on dual-use technology. This reciprocal rule might also include targeting the private communications of defense contractors, politicians, ambassadors, or weapon scientists. As a highly invasive and privacy infringing action, the intelligence officers would need to consider if the intelligence threat from their target is so grave that their own state inhabitants would consent to being collected on in a reciprocal foreign collection as a cost of garnering intelligence. So, for example, agents from Israeli unit 8200 would need to consider if the threat from Iranian nuclear scientists was so grave that Israeli scientists would accept the risk of having their private communications intercepted by Iranian forces as a cost of the Israeli operation.

A further implication of this reciprocal rule follows. The agency heads have to consider their adversary state's technological development and ability, and likely means of reciprocal responses, even if the adversaries are adhering to the security standard and being as rights-respecting as possible. So, for example, if Iranian methods of signal intercepts directed at Israeli scientists are much cruder and more invasive than the boutique methods of Israeli unit 8200, agency heads in Israel would have to consider if that level of intrusion would likely be seen as tolerable among Israelis as a cost of intelligence collection. I think in most cases, it probably would, that most people in a difficult security environment would permit the risk of having private communications intercepted as a cost of collecting on their adversaries.

That said, this rule would rule out collecting in countries that are not a security threat to one's own country, and it would rule out collecting on, say, politicians or ambassadors who have a low likelihood of having security sensitive information. Finally, this reciprocal standard suggests that except in the most desperate security environments, targeting the friends, lovers, or family of intelligence targets for collection—who have not waived nor forfeited their rights—would be prohibited.

4 | The Torture Debate
David Luban

Before I dive into the torture debate, I want to start with some historical reminders.

Before 9/11, Americans didn't support torture. Torture was what the bad guys did. In war movies, Nazis tortured Americans, not the other way around. Cops who used the "third degree" on suspects were bad cops. With no controversy, we joined the international treaty banning torture, and Congress made torture a serious federal crime. In 1980, a U.S. court called torture "dastardly and totally inhuman."[1] During the Reagan administration two Texas sheriffs went to prison for waterboarding a suspect.[2] The Supreme Court said sleep deprivation as an interrogation technique was like the Inquisition of the Middle Ages.[3] Only kooks and provocateurs defended torture, and a book called *The Torture Debate in America* would never have been published, because there *was* no "torture debate in America."

All that changed on a dime after 9/11. Within days newspapers reported that torture was now a kitchen-table conversation topic; college students, polled by their teachers about whether or not to torture terrorists, mostly said yes.

It's obvious what was going on. In the aftershock of 9/11, we were having a national revenge fantasy. Unfortunately it's a fantasy that never went away.

Pretty soon officials were talking about how we needed to go to the dark side, and that the gloves were coming off. The CIA started designing its enhanced interrogation program soon after 9/11, even before we caught the first high-value detainee. Almost every high-level official in the government signed off on it, including the president, vice-president, and SECDEF. Torture opponents like Navy General Counsel Alberto Mora were sidelined in the official rush to the dark side.

There was a brief moment of reckoning after the Abu Ghraib scandal and its shocking photos came to light. But even then, 42 percent of Americans answered "often" and "sometimes" to the question, "Should terrorist suspects be tortured?" Then it came out that Abu Ghraib wasn't just some untrained reserves gone rogue. The same techniques in the Abu Ghraib photos had been used on men in GTMO with official approval.

American pro-torture sentiment never went down. Instead, it climbed. By 2009 it was more than 50 percent. By 2014 it was close to 60 percent. That makes the United States one of the most pro-torture countries in the world, according to several international opinion polls—including a poll in countries involved in ongoing armed conflicts.

I'm mentioning all this to give some context for discussing the issue today. Some context—but also a warning that U.S. popular opinion is an outlier, and it's hardened over the years.

With this as background, let's turn to the torture debate—or, rather, the three torture debates we've had over the last twenty years: the legal debate, the moral debate, and the debate over whether torture works.

LEGAL

I'm going to start with the legal debate—not because it's the most important, but because of an important fact: in one opinion poll, it turned out that a third of pro-torture Americans didn't know torture was against the law, and they said that if they had known, they wouldn't be pro-torture.

Something that I find startling is that when ethicists and politicians debate torture, they always start with ticking-bomb scenarios, and never so much as hint that torture is a serious felony. It carries a twenty-year sentence, and the death penalty if the victim dies. Torture is also a war crime under U.S. law. And that's been true since well before 9/11. Lesser forms of abuse—what the law calls "cruel, inhuman, or degrading treatment"—have been banned since the McCain Amendment in 2005.⁴

More than that, the anti-torture treaty we ratified twenty-five years ago says there are no exceptions, not in wars and not in emergencies.

In that case, how did government lawyers end up approving it? The answer is that they decided that the so-called "enhanced interrogation techniques" (EITs) aren't bad enough to be torture. As defined by law, torture requires *severe* mental or physical pain or suffering.

The government lawyers who approved the EITs did two things. First, they set the bar very high: physical pain or suffering weren't severe unless they were equivalent to the pain or suffering of organ failure or death. Now that's a little weird when you think about it, since nobody knows how painful death is, and not many know how painful organ failure is. One result is that a lawyer briefing GTMO personnel couldn't think of much more to say than "if he dies, you're doing it wrong." When the torture memo went public, an embarrassed DOJ quickly retracted this idea—but they still approved the EITs.

That's because of the second thing the lawyers did: they took the CIA's word that medical personnel would be monitoring the interrogations to make sure they never crossed the severity line. Now that, too, is a little weird. Last year I injured my shoulder. When I went to the doctor, *he* asked *me* how badly it hurt—how did I rate it on a 1-to-10 scale? I didn't ask *him* how badly it hurt, and if I did, he would have thought I was insane. Medicine isn't mind-reading. Medics grading how severe someone else's pain is are only doing fake medicine.

That's not the only thing that's backward about taking the agency's word that medical personnel would ensure that the abuse would never cross the line of permissible severity. To the agency's question about whether the EITs were severe enough to be torture, the lawyers answered, in effect, "they aren't because you say they aren't." That's not a legal opinion—it's a permission slip.

But in their hundreds of pages of argle-bargle, the lawyers never even discussed the most important part of the law. They focused on severe *physical* pain or suffering and asked how severe waterboarding and wall-slamming were, which of course is debatable.

What they forgot is that *mental* torture is also a crime. And one curious fact about U.S. torture law is that while it never defines "severe physical pain or suffering," it *does* define "severe mental pain or suffering." It's the prolonged suffering that comes from procedures calculated to profoundly disrupt the personality. And it turns out that profound personality disruption is exactly what enhanced interrogation is about.

Congress included that clause because our Cold War adversaries used drugs and other "procedures" to brainwash prisoners. And in the 1950s the CIA began researching those same "procedures" in a secret program called "MK Ultra." It included dosing unsuspecting subjects with LSD without their consent. One of them was a scientist named Frank Olson, who ended up jumping out of a window to his death in 1953. In the 1970s all of this came out in a series of Congressional investigations, and it was one of the agency's biggest scandals. President Ford officially apologized to Olson's family.

Other MK Ultra procedures included isolation, sensory deprivation mixed with sensory overload, and more subtle techniques for disorienting victims and wearing them down—the official language was causing "debilitation, dependency, and dread." According to an agency training manual, the goal is to reduce the subject to an "infantile state,"[5] a "loss of autonomy, a reversion to an earlier behavioral level." Today this is called "learned helplessness."

Now movies give us a kind of false idea of what torture interrogation is. The torturer tightens the screws, and the victim finally screams, "Okay! Okay! I'll talk!" That's not the program of debilitation, dependency, and dread. That program consists of heaping one small abuse on top of another.

- Lights on 24/7.
- Then lights off 24/7.
- Don't empty the waste bucket, so the cell stinks.
- Round-the-clock white noise.
- No clocks or windows.
- Wake the prisoner up at irregular times.
- Feed him short rations.
- Make the cell too hot or too cold.
- Keep doing this for weeks on end.

None of these abuses even makes it onto the list of EITs. Then throw in the EITs during the interrogation sessions. After regression and loss of autonomy, subjects can quietly be debriefed.

Now once we see what's really going on, it becomes clear why the torture memos are a complete diversion. All they do is go down the EIT list and ask of every technique whether it inflicts severe pain. That misses the forest for the trees. It's this round-the-clock low-level abuse, with the EITs as icing on the cake, that are "procedures calculated to disrupt profoundly the personality."

And let me repeat the legal punchline: the U.S. Torture Act *defines* this kind of prolonged personality disruption as "severe mental pain or suffering"—that is, mental torture. No need to ask, "How severe is it?" as with physical pain.

TICKING BOMBS

I want to turn next to the moral debate. Ethicists might not care whether torture is legal or not. What they want to know is whether torture is ever morally permitted. Maybe the law gets it wrong: Maybe there *are* cases where torturing prisoners for information is the right thing to do. Those will be cases where the information is necessary to save lives—the "ticking bomb scenario." We all know how that goes: A terrorist has planted a time bomb in a crowded city. We catch him, the bomb is ticking, and he won't talk. Isn't it permissible to torture him to save hundreds of lives? Or millions of lives if it's a nuclear bomb?

And if the answer is "yes," then how about dozens of lives? How about two lives? How about one life? Once you've conceded that torture is morally permissible to save a million lives, you've conceded that torture is, in principle, permissible. Now, as Charles Krauthammer once wrote, "all that's left is to haggle about the price."

The ticking bomb argument for torture can go in two familiar ways. One is to think of it like a Trolley Problem, a numbers game of one versus many. One person's short-term suffering versus another's life, or ten lives, or hundreds of lives. Krauthammer called this a "rational moral calculus," and arguably the cost-benefit analysis favors torture. That's how a card-carrying utilitarian might frame the argument.

The other way the pro-torture argument runs is not utilitarian, but instead is based on the theory of rights forfeiture. In the ticking bomb scenario, either the terrorist suffers or the innocent bomb victims suffer. That's the deadly trade-off, and it's the terrorist's fault. By forcing the trade-off, the terrorist forfeits his right against having suffering inflicted on him.

These are strong arguments, but they both have problems.

One problem with both is that they have a hard time setting limits on torture. If only the numbers count, it doesn't matter whether the person you're torturing is a terrorist or not, as long as you get the information. Why not torture the terrorist's innocent child, if that's the only way to make him talk? Why not rape the child, if that's the only way to make the terrorist talk? If you think that's disgusting and wrong, you aren't really a utilitarian.

Maybe it's because the child has rights that haven't been forfeited. That pushes us toward the rights-forfeiture argument. But it has a similar problem. If the terrorist has forfeited the right against torture, then there is no upper limit on what you can do. If nothing will make them talk except burning or racking or raping—well, morality requires interrogators to burn, rack, and rape. They made themself liable, the bomb victims didn't, and that's the end of the moral story. Perhaps the torture defender would protest that extreme tortures are too hideous to inflict. But that just begs the question of why some tortures are out while others are in.

I have a more basic complaint about the ticking bomb arguments: they're built on hypotheticals that are like cartoons. Look at all the assumptions built in.

- First, you know there's a ticking bomb.
- You know the person you caught knows where it is.
- You know you've got the right person, not someone else with the same name, like in the botched el-Masri case that really happened.
- You know they won't talk until it's too late to disarm the bomb.
- And you're pretty sure they *will* talk if you torture them.
- You're confident they won't give you false information to lead you on a wild goose chase.
- You know you can't find the bomb any other way.
- And you can't evacuate the area.

Well, theorists can assume anything they want; that's what makes theorizing so much fun. They can also assume this torture thing is a one-off in an emergency, not a policy of torturing every high-value suspect you catch—even though that's how the enhanced programs we know about actually work in the countries that use them.

I might add something obvious: the MK Ultra techniques take time to work, and in the ticking bomb scenario, we're assuming that interrogators don't have time.

And let's not assume that torture will be used to the bare minimum necessary. Interrogators have a strong incentive to keep going even after the victim has been drained dry, because there is no way to tell the difference between someone with nothing more to give and someone who's holding out. Langley ordered Abu Zubaydah's interrogators to keep waterboarding him even after the interrogation team thought he had nothing left to tell.

And don't talk about doing it as a reluctant last resort, and only the minimum that's necessary. What we learned from the torture memos is that U.S. interrogators gave detainees only one chance at providing actionable intelligence, before starting the enhanced interrogations.

My suggestion is this: If you want to have a serious moral conversation about torture, then don't talk about ticking time bombs *EVER*. Talk about torture used against terrorist suspects where the interrogators don't know in advance what the suspects know, or even whether they know anything valuable. Talk about torturing people to get small bits of information about safe houses and bank accounts. Talk about countries where torture turned from a rare exception to a routine practice. Talk about reality.

DOES TORTURE WORK?

But I bet you want to know whether torture works. That's the third torture debate, and it often seems it's the only one people really care about—which does not reflect very well on us, but (as the saying goes) it is what it is, and we are who we are.

The first thing to be clear is what we're asking. If the question is "Does torture ever produce reliable information?" the answer is surely yes.

But isn't the right question whether you could have gotten the same information without torture? A lot of experienced interrogators say that rapport building works better. In U.S. experience, it seems that "enhanced" interrogators hardly even tried. One of the revelations in the torture memos is that the high-value captives got only one chance to provide actionable information before enhanced interrogation started.

Obviously you can't do controlled experiments on how well torture works. Experimenting on prisoners is a war crime for good reason. But you can study it indirectly. The neuroscientist Shane O'Mara reviewed the large experimental literature on the effects of stress, sleep deprivation, hunger, and extremes of temperature on memory and cognition. These are the MK Ultra tools, but the experiments were mostly done for unrelated purposes.

The conclusions are consistent and stunning: all of these abuses degrade the ability to recall information.

No doubt people can still remember big events. But real-world interrogation is about phone numbers and email addresses and bank accounts and safe houses. If that's what you want, degrading the subject's ability to remember is to say the least counterproductive. Maybe that's why rapport building gets better information than going to the dark side.

But suppose, for the sake of argument, that torture sometimes produces truthful information that couldn't be gotten any other way. One problem is that along with the truthful information, the victim may give up a boatload of false information, to mislead interrogators, or tell them what they want to hear. If the disinformation sends us on wild goose chases, it can impose real security costs. That happened with one of the sources of false intelligence that helped land us in the Iraq War.

And once word gets out that detainees are being tortured, potential informants might be afraid to come forward. So even if torture works, the net result might be less useful information, not more. And torture can turn into a recruitment tool for terrorists. Abu Ghraib poured gasoline on the Iraq insurgency.

Let me be clear. Nothing I've just said *proves* that torture doesn't work. Proof is out of the question when everything's secret and intelligence agencies and victims both have incentives to lie.

What I'm suggesting instead is to keep your eyes on the real prize: national security. The right pragmatic question isn't "Does torture work?" It's "Does torture help national security?" And in the torture debates that hardly ever gets asked.

I hope it's clear by now that I think the focus on whether torture works is a badly defined question. And I think it's the wrong question—in a much more profound way. We only get to that question once we push morality and law aside. That's something we should never do. John McCain said, "This is not about the terrorists. It is about us."[6] He was right.

NOTES

1. *Filartiga v. Pena-Irala*, 630 F.2d 876, 883 (2d Cir. 1980).
2. *U.S. v. Lee*, 744 F.2d 1124 (5th Cir. 1984).
3. *Ashcraft v. Tennessee*, 322 U.S. 143, 150 n.8 (1944).
4. 42 U.S.C. §2000dd. Strengthened in §2000dd–2.
5. CIA KUBARK Manual (July 1963), p. 41.
6. https://fas.org/irp/congress/2011_cr/torture.html.

5 | Technology and the Moral Limits of Intelligence Collection
C. Anthony Pfaff

INTRODUCTION

In January 2020 United Nations experts recommended an investigation into the possibility Saudi Arabia had introduced spyware into the phone of Amazon CEO Jeff Bezos via a WhatsApp message sent from an account associated with Crown Prince Muhammad Bin Salman. The purpose, the experts concluded, was to facilitate a "massive online campaign" against Bezos who also owns the *Washington Post*. Prior to the hack, the *Post* had published several articles associating the Crown Prince with the brutal murder of journalist Jamal Khashoggi. Bezos himself suggested that it was the Saudis who leaked information about an extramarital affair to U.S. tabloids.[1]

There is, of course, no need to entertain the question whether hacking Bezos' phone to blackmail him was ethical or not. Suppressing free speech to cover up a murder fails at so many levels it is not worth asking. However, it is worth asking if it was impermissible to collect on Bezos at all? That question is the more difficult question to answer. National security-related information does not only reside with the government and its employees. Amazon, for example, had bid on a contract to provide the Department of Defense to develop the Joint Enterprise Defense Infrastructure, which would provide cloud-computing resources to the Department. While they did not get the contract, it is not hard to imagine adversaries having a legitimate security interest in the program and determining Amazon may have information related to that interest.[2] It is now worth asking, given a legitimate security interest, would one want to place limits on such collection?

Consider, for example, the app ToTok, which the Emirati government reportedly uses to track conversations, movements, relationships, appointments, and images of those who use it. To encourage its use, the Emiratis have restricted access to competitors like WhatsApp and Skype, in effect coercing anyone in the country who relies on chat apps to use it. ToTok, however, is not limited to the Emirates. It has been widely downloaded in the United States as well, extending the reach of Emirati intelligence services.[3] To the extent the Emiratis rely on the app to collect on legitimate threats, it remains an open question whether it is unethical, despite the anticompetitive practices they employ to encourage its use.

Cyber and communications technologies are not the only concern. Artificial intelligence (AI) is increasingly relied on to make decisions regarding intelligence collection. Project Maven, for example, incorporates computer vision and machine learning algorithms to analyze visual data and identify possible hostile activity, in effect making decisions about what information collected is evidence of a threat.[4] It is not hard to imagine future applications that use that analysis to drive collection, thus making decisions about whom to target for collection, how to target them for collection, and why. It is one thing to rely on machines to sort through a crowd to find particular individuals; however, it does not follow that one should rely on machines to determine what to do with those persons once found. Perhaps more to the point in the context of intelligence gathering, does it make moral sense to develop machines that are also adept at lying, cheating, and stealing, which characterize intelligence collection?[5]

One of the problems in addressing these concerns is that mass surveillance technologies do not just affect the needle they are looking for; rather, they affect the whole haystack, as well. In short, by creating a panoptic effect where everyone has reason to believe they are being surveilled, these technologies can have a coercive effect where persons restrict their social interactions based on what they prefer to keep private and their beliefs about the government's expectations regarding their behavior. China, of course, has given the world a glimpse of the extreme through its social scoring system, which couples mass surveillance with social expectations, which enables it to enforce conformity on a large scale. However, in avoiding the extreme, it is equally important not to lose the value these technologies have toward meeting basic physical and national security needs. Finding the right balance requires understanding the role consent plays as individuals and governments negotiate the practical aspects of the social contract.

ESPIONAGE AND TECHNOLOGY

Getting those answers right depends a lot on context: it matters who is spying, on whom they are spying, and why. State actors have different obligations to their own citizens than to the citizens of other states by virtue of the social contract. So while a mass surveillance program by the U.S. government against its own citizens might be rights violating, a similar program directed at an adversary may not be.[6] In part, this permission makes sense because a government, generally, does not have the ability to impose mass conformity on a foreign society the way it can on its own. However, because knowledge of such systems does have coercive effect, there will still be limits on the extent to which such surveillance should go.

For the purposes of this discussion, I will focus exclusively on foreign espionage efforts, where espionage is understood as "an attempt to penetrate an adversarial system for purposes of extracting sensitive or protected information."[7] What distinguishes espionage from other forms of collection, at least for the purposes of this discussion, is its reliance on deception, theft, and law-breaking, at least of the state where it is undertaken. In this regard, technology does not necessarily pose a new moral problem. Successful espionage has always relied on deceiving potential sources regarding one's identity and intent, taking of information against an owner's will, and violating the laws of the country in which espionage is conducted. Worse yet, it also often involves convincing others to not only engage in these otherwise unethical acts, but to betray their country as well.[8]

Also, I will focus on the ethics of collecting the information itself independently from what one does with the information to focus on the ethical limits of technology more clearly, even when the purpose of that information is further intelligence collection. It is one thing, for example, to collect on someone's communications, and another to use what one finds out to blackmail that person into becoming a source. For the latter, the real question is whether blackmail in those circumstances is permissible, not so much whether it was permissible to collect in the first place.

So, what's different? Maybe not as much as one might think, at least from a moral perspective. However, as the Bezos case illustrates, technology has expanded the range of persons and information it is useful to target and collect. Consider the Chinese theft of information at the Office of Personnel Management (OPM) back in 2015. In the theft, they were able to obtain the security clearance applications of everyone who had applied for a clearance through OPM. Since intelligence agencies do not use OPM to process clearances, it is possible the Chinese were able to identify which U.S. personnel were likely involved in intelligence operations.[9]

ESPIONAGE AND ETHICS

Of course, it is not unethical for states to root out spies. More to the point, there is nothing inherently unethical about spying. Whether one subscribes to Hobbes or Locke, by virtue of the social contract, citizens have a right to expect their government to protect them from external threat, and governments have a responsibility to do so. In that light, there may be nothing wrong with China's OPM hack. Does it matter that the Chinese government has personal information about American citizens if they do not do anything with it? It does not seem that the Chinese government has used the OPM information to blackmail, extort, or punish Americans as the Saudis may have with Bezos.

Ross W. Bellaby answers this question, in part at least, in his application of Jeremy Bentham's panopticon. Originally intended as a prison design, the panopticon is a system of control that places "guards" in a central tower which is then ringed by cells, in which the prisoners live. Thus, the guards can always see the prisoners, but not the other way around. Thus, prisoners would never know if they were being watched, but always had reason to believe they were. As a result, they would conform their behavior to the guards' wishes. Foucault, as Bellaby notes, seized on the idea as a metaphor for institutional power that induces conformity. Technology has transformed metaphor into digital reality.

Bellaby's point here is that the panoptic gaze interferes with individuals' autonomy. People alter their behavior when they believe they are being watched, and in Foucault's view, they do so to comply with what they think the watchers want from them.[10] Of course, in the context of intelligence collection, the issue is not conformity as much as it is about protecting one's own information. The effect of digital technologies entails one does not know when one is being watched nor does one know what information is useful, or how its use will be harmful. Russians, for example, collect data on millions of social media users to conduct tailored disinformation campaigns aimed at undermining Western institutions.[11]

In this way, the panoptic gaze of mass surveillance technologies compels anonymity and caution regarding how communications technologies are used. It also causes a pervasive sense of vulnerability precisely because they are certain they are being watched but are uncertain how they should behave. So, when it comes to personal information, persons under the panoptic gaze cannot be sure regarding what they should protect or how. While certainly forcing persons into such anonymity is a harm, it is also somewhat self-defeating as it incentivizes behavior that undermines the surveillance's effectiveness. Infringing on other's autonomy in a self-defeating way is not only unethical, it is irrational. Finding a way ahead thus requires finding a way to collect intelligence in a way that respects other's autonomy.

AN ETHICAL FRAMEWORK FOR JUST INTELLIGENCE COLLECTION

Just intelligence is not just war. Part of the problem in finding a way ahead is that much of the literature on intelligence ethics tries to assimilate it into the just war tradition.[12] Doing so should not be surprising. Intelligence collection is often motivated by the existence of a threat, which can place rights regarding property, privacy, and autonomy in tension with others' rights to life and liberty. Of course, most who argue for applying the just war tradition will acknowledge that much of intelligence collection is dedicated to finding threats, rather than responding to them.

So, unlike just war theory, which only differentiates between combatants and noncombatants and only really accounts for one kind of harm—death—they recognize that permissions regarding intelligence collection can vary based on target and harm. Bellaby, for example, argues for a "ladder of escalation" which correlates level of harm with level of justification: the greater the threat, the greater the harms permitted.[13] While Bellaby does argue for some kind of discrimination between permissible and impermissible targets, like just war theory, he assumes that legitimate targets are already assimilated into the category of "threat." But this seems to ignore whether the subjects of this harm *deserved* it or not. That is because the identity of the subject does not matter as long as the principles of just intelligence, which include just cause, proportionality, authority, and discrimination are fulfilled.

The problem here is the just war tradition is an ethic for enemies. However, as Tamara Meisels points out, the enemy relationship is not inherently exploitive. Drawing on Parfit, she notes that we do not use people when we defend ourselves against their attack. In fact, in war, our aims are better served if the enemy isn't even there.[14] In the course of destroying the enemy, there may be occasion for exploitation. But we do not exploit the enemy: we kill, destroy, neutralize, or otherwise harm them.

So, if we want to get at an ethic of intelligence, we have to understand it as an ethic of exploitation; and an ethic of exploitation requires an understanding of how consent both constrains and enables permissions regarding how we treat other persons.

EXPLOITATION AND CONSENT

Consent is a central moral criterion on evaluating one's behavior toward others. Murders, thefts, and lies can all be recognized to be wrong, in part because they are violations of consent: no one consents to be murdered or to have one's goods stolen. Should one consent to such things, those acts would no longer count as "murder" or "theft" at all. Consent plays such a critical role in moral reasoning because it is the manifestation of the freedom of the person. Kant recognized this in one of his formulations of his famous categorical imperative: "Act in such a way that you always treat humanity, whether in your own person or in the person of another, never simply as a means, but always at the same time as an end."[15]

Failure to abide by someone else's consent entails treating that person as a nonperson, more like a tool than a user, simply a means to one's ends rather than as self-determining agents capable of choosing their own ends. In Kantian terms, treating someone as a self-determining agent, or an "end," is synonymous with respecting the dignity of that person's freedom. Treating others as an end and not merely a means requires one to adopt a stance toward fellow human beings that demands moral impartiality. It requires that we recognize the limits another's refusal to consent entails for our conduct.

Consent, however, does not entail preference. To make this point clearer, consider an analogy from a football game and the shared expectations that result from those engaged in the playing of the game. These "shared expectations" are the rules of the game consented to by both the players and the spectators of the game, though in importantly different ways. Consonant with the rules, both teams may attempt to deceive each other even though this is clearly using the other as a means. But since nothing interferes with their choice to play the game, they are also being respected as ends (i.e., not used *merely* as means). In this context, the fact that one team is completely overwhelmed by some deception is not the fault of the deceiving team, but of the deceived team for failing to play well by discerning and counteracting the other team's strategy.[16]

Failure to abide by the rules of the game, however, will result in the end of the game itself. Hence, certain kinds of conduct in the game are impermissible, conduct that contradicts the conditions on which the game's being played. But it is conduct that undermines the playing of the game for *both* sides, akin to the golden rule ethical principles articulated earlier. Any kind of conduct that results in such self-defeat, in the de facto cessation of the game, is irrational relative to the game. Any kind of conduct in intelligence-gathering that results in self-defeat, in the de facto cessation of respect for the other party's (and, derivatively, *my side's*) free agency, is likewise irrational relative to the ethics of intelligence.

As the game analogy suggests, different persons can be subject to different harms in different circumstances. Quarterbacks, for example, can only be tackled when they have the ball. Players who do not have the ball, on the other hand, can be hit in order to block them, for example, from tackling the person who has the ball. What also follows from this analogy is that participation is not limited to players, so neither are harms, though they are much more limited. Opposing coaches and spectators may not be tackled, but they can be deceived regarding things such as what play one will actually run.

Espionage is enabled by the consent of individual citizens seeking the protection of their governments. In seeking this protection, they impose a responsibility on the government to engage in, among other things, intelligence activities to identify threats from which they need to be protected. So, some people may join the game as spectators, while others join the game as players, but joining is something that everyone does insofar as he is a citizen at all.[17]

So rather than correlating harms to justification, it is better to correlate harms to consent. Of course, it is important to be clear what one is consenting to. Football players may consent, under certain circumstances, to be tackled, but they do not consent to just any physical contact. Pulling face masks, hitting someone before they've caught the ball, and so on are considered interference, and thus count as cheating.

For the purpose of ethical analysis, intelligence activities can be assessed on a spectrum of invasiveness, where at one end would be passive collection activities that review information that would, in principle, at least be public like CCTV cameras in a bank lobby. On the other extreme, there is malware or other surveillance technologies that target specific individuals and systems to gain full access to whatever information they might contain.

The first category of legitimate targets of intelligence gathering are government and corporate systems and personnel involved in national security. These persons are subject to the most invasive forms of intelligence gathering since they are most fully "players" in the game. They should, by virtue of their access, be aware of having their communications surveilled as well as the means to protect themselves.

The second category of legitimate targets of intelligence gathering is government and corporate systems and personnel not involved in national security. In general, this analysis would suggest they would be subject to passive collection to determine whether national security–related information has somehow crossed over, but not more invasive measures. However, as the OPM and Russian trolling examples suggest, this judgment mistakes what counts as relevant national security information. This point suggests that there is a burden on the government to protect a wider range of information that it collects and stores.

That burden does not entail classifying a wider range of information, but it does suggest an ethical obligation to invest in means to protect that information. Still, not everyone who joins the government is involved in national security and thus should not be subject to the panoptic gaze. This point entails that while nonsecurity related entities may be subject to invasive collection when relevant information is found through passive means, collecting nonrelated information would count as unethical. Of course, at some level one has to look at all the information to determine what is of value, but what would be wrong would be to collect and store nonsecurity-related information.

The third category of intelligence target is the ordinary citizen. As already discussed, as citizens, they participate in "the game" though in a very limited capacity. The question is, "What does that limited capacity enable?" Seamus Miller and Patrick Walsh point out in their discussion regarding the NSA collection techniques leaked by Snowden, there is a difference between privacy and anonymity. Privacy is the right to control information about oneself, including how and when one is perceived by others. Anonymity, on the other hand, is when one's identity is concealed to another. Anonymity may be instrumental to privacy, but it does not constitute privacy. Moreover, privacy is closely related to autonomy since some level of privacy is required for persons to pursue their projects and interests without interference from others.[18]

So, if there is no right to anonymity, then there would be few prohibitions on collecting information just because it contains basic information regarding identity or activities one does in public spaces. As an ethical permission, though, all this is really saying, is that anything one does in public one should not expect to keep private. Having said that, technology complicates the matter as it allows those activities not just to be collected, but also stored. It is less clear that just because persons engage in public activity, that they also agree that it be recorded. This is not some abstract concern associated with perfect voyeurism. The Chinese government may not have done anything unethical with the massive amount of personal data it obtained on U.S. citizens, but that does not mean others, such as criminal elements, will not get access. This point suggests that a measure such as the European Union's General Data Protection Regulation that includes a "right to be forgotten" not only serves as a way of protecting privacy, it also serves as a counterintelligence measure, as it restricts information an adversary might otherwise be able to collect.[19] This also does suggest that there should be a conversation regarding what sort of information is stored by providers such that it would be subject to collection in the first place.

But there is private space, so when does one "consent" to the possibility of being subject to intelligence collection? As Adam Diderichsen and Kira Vrist Rønn point out, consent depends on four key elements: it is active, rational, good, and public. It is active in that it depends on something one says or does; it is rational in that one should have good reasons for giving that consent; good in the sense that there is no evidence of mental deficiency or coercion; and public in that persons know what they are consenting to.[20]

This last element is the one that primarily concerns us here. Consent, for it to matter in this discussion, should be informed. That means as persons enter the digital space, they should be reasonably aware of how their information will be used and interpreted in the same way those participating in a football game know what the rules are. The problem for digital space, of course, is it is not clear that there are rules. In response, Diderichsen and Rønn further argue for a more open discussion concerning the various elements in the intelligence toolbox to enable clear legislation and accountability as well as more public information regarding the criteria for deeming what sort of information is relevant to national security or not.[21]

CONCLUSION

If the game analogy holds, then the takeaway may be that to some degree technology is changing the rules of the game. By exposing a wider range of persons and information to collection, it challenges previously held norms regarding autonomy, privacy, and the limits of foreign intelligence collection. As such, technology imposes additional burdens on both collectors and their targets. Thus governments, as representatives of both classes, should invest in means that adequately discriminate relevant and nonrelevant information as well as engage in public discussions regarding what is permissible.

But this is how one breaks the pernicious effects of the panoptic gaze. First, it is important to be clear what it is for and use it for only those purposes. Even prisoners want protection from external threats. But to secure the gaze from inevitable abuse, persons need to retain at least some control over what it sees. In this way, its self-defeating dynamic can be broken.

Acting morally does not necessarily mean states must give up obtaining critical information, but it does mean they may have to give up certain ways of obtaining it, even if that means intelligence officers must take greater risks. In practical terms this means intelligence professionals must take care in determining the nature, as well as the targets, of their operations. In terms of the nature of their operations, these are limited only by the collective self-defense conditions that make it possible and morally permissible to play the intelligence game in the first place. In terms of the targets of their operations, this means they may only target those who have voluntarily entered the game and avoid involving people who may be useful, but who have not, by any choice they have made, involved themselves.

NOTES

1. Charles Riley and Shimon Prokupecz, "UN Calls for investigation after Saudi Crown Prince Implicated in Hack of Jeff Bezos' Phone," CNN, January 23, 2020, https://www.cnn.com/2020/01/22/tech/jeff-bezos-mbs-phone-hack/index.html, accessed February 6, 2020.
2. Jay Greene and Aaron Gregg, "Amazon will Challenge Pentagon's Award of $10 Billion JEDI Contract to Microsoft," *Washington Post*, November 14, 2019, https://www.washingtonpost.com/business/2019/11/14/amazon-will-challenge-pentagons-award-billion-jedi-contract-microsoft/, accessed February 7, 2020.
3. Mark Mazzetti, Nicole Perlroth, and Ronen Bergman, "It Seemed like a Popular Chat App. It's Secretly a Spy Tool," *New York Times*, December 22, 2019, https://www.nytimes.com/2019/12/22/us/politics/totok-app-uae.html, accessed February 6, 2020.
4. Kelsey D. Atherton, "Targeting the Future of the DOD's Controversial Project Maven Initiative," *C4ISRNET*, July 27, 2018, https://www.c4isrnet.com/it-networks/2018/07/27/targeting-the-future-of-the-dods-controversial-project-maven-initiative/, accessed February 9, 2020.
5. Patrick Lin and Shannon Ford, "I, spy robot: The ethics of robots in national intelligence activities," in *Ethics and the Future of Spying: Technology, National Security, and Intelligence Collection* (London: Routledge, 2016), 150.

6. Mark Jensen, "The Virtues of Bond and Vices of Bauer: An Aristotelian Defense of Espionage," *Ethics and the Future of Spying: Technology, National Security, and Intelligence Collection* (London: Routledge, 2016), 16.

7. Thomas Rid, "Cyber war will not take place," *Journal of Strategic Studies* 35, no. 1 (2012), 20.

8. David L. Perry, *Partly Cloudy* (Lanham, MD: Scarecrow Press, 2009), 104.

9. Evan Perez, "U.S. pulls spies from China after hack," *CNN*, September 15, 2015, https://money.cnn.com/2015/09/30/technology/china-opm-hack-us-spies/index.html, accessed February 7, 2020.

10. Ross W. Bellaby, *The Ethics of Intelligence: A New Framework* (New York: Routledge Press, 2014), 77.

11. Massimo Calabresi, "Russia's social media war on America," *Time*, May 18, 2017, https://www.csis.org/features/russias-attacks-democratic-justice-systems, accessed February 9, 2020. Suzanne Spaulding, Devi Nair, and Arthur Nelson, *Attacks on Democratic Justice Systems* (Washington, DC: CSIS, 2019), https://www.csis.org/features/russias-attacks-democratic-justice-systems, accessed February 9, 2020.

12. Bellaby, *The Ethics of Intelligence*, 24.

13. Bellaby, *The Ethics of Intelligence*, 31–34.

14. Tamara Meisels, "Kidnapping and Extortion as Tactics of Soft War," in Michael Gross and Tamara Meisels, ed., *Soft War: The Ethics of Unarmed Conflict* (Cambridge: Cambridge University Press, 2017), 214.

15. Immanuel Kant [ca. 1785], *Groundwork of the Metaphysics of Morals*, trans. H. J. Patton (New York: Harper and Row, 1964), 96.

16. John Mark Mattox, "The moral limits of military deception," *Journal of Military Ethics*, 1, no. 1 (2002), 9–12.

17. Charles A. Pfaff and Jeffrey Tiel, "The ethics of espionage," *Journal of Military Ethics*, 1, no. 3 (2004), 1–15.

18. Seumas Miller and Patrick Walsh, "The NSA Leaks, Edward Snowden, and the Ethics and Accountability of Intelligence," in *Ethics and the Future of Spying: Technology, National Security, and Intelligence Collection* (New York: Routledge, 2016), 194.

19. Fact Sheet on the "Right to Be Forgotten" ruling (C-131/12), *European Commission*, https://www.inforights.im/media/1186/cl_eu_commission_factsheet_right_to_be_forgotten.pdf, accessed February 9, 2020.

20. Adam Diderichsen and Kira Vrist Rønn, "Intelligence by consent: on the inadequacy of Just War Theory as a framework for intelligence ethics," *Intelligence and National Security*, 32, no. 4 (2017), 486–87.

21. Diderichsen and Rønn, "Intelligence by consent," 488.

6 | Ethical Reflections on Human Intelligence (HUMINT) Gathering
Professor Sir David Omand

Expanded version of a talk given to the U.S. Naval Academy, Annapolis, April 15, 2021, by Professor Sir David Omand, GCB, Visiting Professor in War Studies, King's College London, and former UK Security and Intelligence Coordinator

Secret intelligence gathered by spies has been part of the human story from Old Testament times,[1] as the book of Joshua relates, "Joshua, son of Nun, secretly sent out two men as spies. He told them, 'Go, look at that country, especially the city of Jericho.' So they went to Jericho and entered the house of a prostitute named Rahab to spend the night there."[2]

    I start, therefore, with a reminder of the primary purpose of gathering intelligence which has not changed over the centuries. It is to improve the quality of decision-making by reducing the ignorance of the decision makers of the dangers they face, be they military commanders like Joshua, or presidents and prime ministers today and their policy advisers. Some of what these decision makers need to know as an essential input to many of their choices, is information that their adversaries certainly do not want them to have, and may go to very violent lengths to keep from them. That is the purpose of secret intelligence—reducing the ignorance of the decision makers in respect of information that others wish to conceal from them. Information that has to be stolen: at first by spies, and later by interception of secret messages and diplomatic dispatches, and most recently by a variety of technical means. The well-placed human agent remains, however, the surest way into the mind of the adversary.

Who are those adversaries? They are the hostile dictators and autocrats and their armed forces, terrorists, narcotics traffickers, cyber, and other organized international criminal gangs, all intent on doing things that will harm us. They will go to extraordinary, often violent, lengths to prevent us accessing the secrets of their capabilities, identities and associates, location, movements, financing, and, above all, their plans and intentions. The inhabitants of the peaceful city of Salisbury in England learned this in 2018 when Russian military intelligence sent two assassins to kill Lieutenant Colonel Skripal, a former GRU officer who had successfully spied for MI6, the UK's Secret Intelligence Service. They used a banned military-grade nerve agent Novichok to try to kill Skripal and his daughter, but only succeeded in killing an innocent bystander. We need protection from such people. For that, secret intelligence is indispensable.

That in turn means equipping intelligence officers with the means to overcome the will of the person with the secret, who is determined not to give it up. Intelligence professionals have always argued, therefore, that their difficult and sometimes dangerous job, one that they exercise on our behalf, requires us to accept they will break normal ethical conventions. Without some exceptional ethical license we will acquire no secret intelligence, by definition.

By ethics here I mean the straightforward dictionary definition of ethics as "a social, religious, or civil code of behaviour considered correct, especially that of a particular group, profession or individual." Having an ethical code of conduct is a defining condition for a profession in a democracy. We do not expect teachers to seduce their students, lawyers to embezzle their clients' money, scientists to fiddle the results of their experiments, or military officers to disregard the Geneva conventions governing armed conflict. The issue is how far we want to go in licensing an ethical code for our intelligence professionals, those that we employ to gather intelligence on our behalf, different from that we apply to ourselves in everyday life. What *don't* our citizens want intelligence officers to be allowed to do on their behalf in trying to keep them safe and secure?[3]

There is a recognizable parallel with the centuries old just war tradition that has sought to reconcile conflicting ethical requirements over the use of armed force and that has led to the development of "laws of war" such as today we find in the Geneva Conventions. States have a duty to defend their citizens and justice. Protecting the innocent sometimes requires willingness to use force against those who use violence against them. But we know that deliberately taking or harming human life is morally wrong. Just war thinking reconciles these tensions by insisting that the causes of war must be just (*jus ad bellum*) before armed force is used, and that once engaged in armed conflict our behaviour must be just (*jus in bello*) under an ethical (and now international legal) code that seeks to minimize unnecessary suffering, for example, through a duty to try to protect innocent civilians and to accept the surrender of enemy combatants and vessels.[4]

For the just conduct of intelligence that we might by analogy term *jus in intelligentio*,[5] we can also derive ethical principles from the just war tradition that can be of practical use in the management and oversight of secret intelligence activity. Let me mention six such principles. They should not be thought of as a tick-box list, but as guides to help untangle the sometimes-complex ethical issues that intelligence activity can generate. These principles can be used to think about modern *digital* intelligence, including bulk access to data on fiber-optic cables and hacking into mobile devices and computer networks, activity that bristles with ethical issues over invasions of privacy,[6] but here I focus on human intelligence and the ethical risks that arise with agents or covert human intelligence sources (CHIS) as they are called in the UK. We should remember, however, that today the ideal well-placed agent may be someone with good access to the IT and communications systems of the adversary rather than the traditional recruitment target of a diplomat or intelligence official. Digital and human intelligence are no longer in separate boxes.

The six just war–derived ethical principles that I suggest may be useful are

- *Right intention*: acting with integrity and honesty, and having no hidden political or other agendas behind the authorization or conduct of intelligence activity, or the impartial analysis and presentation of intelligence judgments to decision makers. We saw that important principle called into question in the controversy over the justification of the invasion of Iraq in 2003 and the use of inflated intelligence estimates on supposed Iraqi WMD by the United States and UK in the run-up to the war.

- *Proportionality*: keeping the ethical risks of operations in line with the seriousness of the harm that the operations are intended to mitigate. To give an extreme example, it has been reported by a respected BBC journalist that one of the top British Army agents inside the Provisional IRA during the height of their terrorist campaign was the man whose job was to root out informers inside PIRA, torture them to confess, then execute them, and dump their bodies.[7] It would be a huge ethical and reputational risk to have such a violent criminal as your covert human intelligence source or agent. But the stakes were high. Intelligence from sources inside PIRA was needed about their internal debates. Such intelligence would have confirmed that some in PIRA leadership were coming to the conclusion that they could not achieve their Republican aims through violence and were looking for a way forward without surrendering. Would British prime ministers Margaret Thatcher and then John Major and Tony Blair have had the confidence to let secret backchannel discussions with terrorists continue, part of the path that led to the successful peace process in Northern Ireland, without high-grade intelligence that they were not being deceived? The proportionality judgment is a fine one. It is quite likely, too, that the motive of any active terrorist in offering to cooperate with the authorities would be selfish, to obtain a get-out-of-jail card to avoid prosecution for past crimes. Should such an inducement be offered? The local police in some countries have been known to tip off intelligence officers stationed in friendly embassies when they caught a Soviet or North Korean diplomat drunk driving or in other disreputable behavior that might get them sent back home to face disgrace, or worse, for them and their families—is it ethically acceptable to offer to have the individual released without charge if he agrees to cooperate, or is that a form of blackmail?

- *Right authority*: the more ethically risky the operation, the higher the level of command authority that should be required. The principle of right authority provides for accountability for decisions, proper oversight of the operation, and an audit trail of who agreed to what—essential to defend the reputation of the service when things go wrong, as they are bound to do from time to time. Good practice here is to have sign-off also from an experienced officer of the service, but not in the direct chain of command, acting as an ethical supervisor or counselor over issues such as when an agent might be allowed to participate in a criminal act to maintain their cover. Collusion in wrongdoing is an ethical risk almost always associated with the recruitment of agents within terrorist and major criminal organizations, yet the information such active participants can provide may be the most likely to save lives. Any newcomer into the gang may well be required by the gang leader to commit a serious offense to ensure there is no going back. We saw that with foreign fighters in the so-called Islamic State. And even if an agent in place were to be recruited and provide useful information the case officer will not know what they are doing when out of the case officer's sight—can a U.S. or British government really run as an agent, an individual who is committing murder or robbing banks?

- *A reasonable prospect of success*: originally intended in the just war tradition to prevent vainglorious operations that placed soldiers in unnecessary peril, this principle is about having adequate justification for imposing serious risk on others. At a time of East/West confrontation MI6 and CIA were jointly running GRU Colonel Oleg Penkovsky in Moscow. He provided thousands of pages of documents, including a description of how Soviet medium-range missile bases would be constructed that provided crucial clues during the Cuban Missile Crisis that the missile sites were not yet operational. That gave President Kennedy just enough time to impose the successful naval blockade of Cuba and defuse the situation. But there was heavy pressure to obtain even more intelligence from Penkovsky, who was prepared to take big risks to help the West, and that may have led to lapses in tradecraft that led to his exposure, arrest, and torture. He died reportedly being thrust alive into a furnace with the film of this shown to GRU colleagues as a warning of what happens to traitors to the Soviet Union. Indeed, after the failed 2018 attempt by GRU assassins to kill former MI6 agent Colonel Skripal in Salisbury, a video emerged of President Putin in an address in Moscow reiterating the threat that "traitors would kick the bucket."[8]

- *Discrimination*: meaning the ability to assess and manage the risk of collateral harm to those not the object of the operation. This ethical principle has particular relevance to digital intelligence today with the ability of

AI algorithms to be applied to bulk data to separate out material relevant to authorized intelligence inquiries from that relating to the innocent Internet user of no interest to the intelligence agencies. But collateral harm can also be an issue in human intelligence activity. What, for example, do we think today of the ethics of the CIA during the Vietnam War in setting up a front company Air America to transport opium base for the poppy-growing Hmong Hill people of Laos in return for their valuable cooperation (and using the proceeds of the drug trafficking to pay for their operations) when some of that heroin would have been likely to end up in the United States, contributing to the major drug abuse problem?

- Finally, *neccessity*: finding no other reasonable way to achieve the authorized mission at lesser ethical risk, for example, by using technical means, given that human agent operations generally carry higher ethical risk. This is particularly true of agent operations against terrorist and organized criminal networks. But sometimes there is no other way of getting the information, other than taking the risk of running human agents, and that can also bring danger for the case officer. A tragic example was that of Captain Robert Nairac who worked undercover for a British Army intelligence unit in Northern Ireland in 1977. He was kidnapped by the Provisional IRA from a bar in the "bandit territory" of South Armagh, when he was waiting to meet his agent, and severely beaten before being shot. We know from other sources that he stayed silent to protect the lives of his agents to whom he had given his word. He was awarded a posthumous George Cross. His body has never been found.

―――◊◊◊◊◊◊◊◊―――

Ethical dilemmas also arise when receiving or sharing intelligence with countries that take different moral attitudes to the gathering and use of intelligence, and to torture and coercive interrogation of terrorist or other suspects. UK judges have made clear that evidence obtained in circumstances where there is a reasonable suspicion that it was obtained under torture will never be admissible in court. UK intelligence officers may, however, if the information is likely to bear on the security of the UK, receive it and follow it up, but are prohibited from participating in, soliciting, encouraging, or condoning the use of torture or cruel, inhuman, or degrading treatment (CIDT), or punishment for any purpose. In no circumstance will UK personnel ever take action amounting to torture or CIDT.[9] Analysts, too, have to have regard to ethics—how certain should analysts be and in what terms should they express the likelihood associated with their estimate, before issuing a report giving, for example, the geolocation of a terrorist leader during an armed conflict when the next step might be a kinetic strike or special forces operation?

At this point, perhaps we should ask a moral philosopher for advice on how to apply ethical principles to constructing an ethical code for those involved in secret intelligence. They are likely to cite three schools of thought.

First, the *consequentialist* (or teleological) tradition—judging the rightness of an act by its consequences—for example, justifying intrusive surveillance that led to a terrorist attack being stopped. Intelligence officers are understandably natural consequentialists, not least since this approach fits with their inclination to continue with operations that generate good results and stop when they don't pay off. But if the threat is really grave, a dirty bomb known to be ticking away somewhere in a city center, for example, would that justify torturing a suspect to reveal where it was? That is the case for drawing on a preexisting ethical code from outside the intelligence world, based on wider religious or ethical teachings.

There is the *deonotological* tradition that would import rules from outside into the ethical code of intelligence officers—an example would be the absolute ban on torture to be found in the UN Declaration on Human Rights, signed by the vast majority of nations and incorporated into the European Convention on Human Rights and the UK's own Human Rights Act. The ethical issue of the "ticking bomb," for example, can then be thought of as being covered by domestic law prohibiting torture arrived at by democratic choice. The British intelligence community prides itself on operating in accordance with UK domestic law. For U.S. agencies that would be equivalent to a requirement to operate in accordance with the U.S. Constitution.

And there is also a third approach that moral philosophers would cite, the so-called *aretaic* tradition, often known as the school of personal value ethics—a way of thinking about how decent human beings *should* behave toward each other, including respect for another's humanity, and not just using other people as a means to your end. Intelligence officers have to work in secret, and sometimes alone overseas, and in conditions of stress and danger. It is down to the personal value ethics of the individual officer whether they behave properly when not being overseen, whatever the rules might say. So, recruiting and training intelligence officers to have a robust internal moral compass is important, just as it is for officers in the Navy, Marine Corps, Army, and Air Force. Aretaic considerations should, for example, lead intelligence officers to feel a sense of moral responsibility for the safety of their agents and their families (and, although not an ethical point, for a human intelligence service to have a reputation for managing well that duty of care can be an important factor in their ability to recruit well-placed agents).

But case officers do still in the end have to recruit and manage agents displaying the full spectrum of personalities, not all likeable, as well quite possibly having psychological troubles. Ask a former CIA or National Clandestine Service officer and they will reply, "Look for weaknesses as encapsulated by the acronym, MICE (money, ideology, coercion/compromise (in other words blackmail) and ego/excitement)." So, case officers have to be trained in psychology and to be able, not cynically but when necessary and proportionate, to manipulate the feelings of others. And counterintelligence officers, likewise, have to have the same understanding to spot the spies in our own ranks.

In the period before and during World War II, ideology—a belief that Soviet communism was the real bulwark against fascism—motivated agents working for the Soviet Union who, like Philby, penetrated British intelligence or the atom bomb spies inside the Manhattan project. That ideological justification waned rapidly with the continued Soviet occupation of Eastern Europe, the 1956 Soviet brutal suppression of the Hungarian uprising, and then the 1968 Soviet invasion of Czechoslovakia, and the crushing of the Prague Spring reform movement. During the later Cold War, the Soviet Union and its Warsaw Pact allies had very few ideological recruits attracted by the Soviet communist system and had to resort to offering large sums of money to recruit those of weak character, like Rick Ames, in the CIA, and exploiting personality weaknesses such as the bipolar disorder of Robert Hanssen of the FBI. Entrapping Western diplomats and business executives visiting the Soviet Union and Eastern Europe in sexual honey traps and subsequently blackmailing them to cooperate or face exposure, became a major tactic for Soviet, East German, and Czech services.[10]

Blackmail, by the way, is not a method to be recommended for agent recruitment. Apart from ethical concerns, the person blackmailed will spend every waking moment trying to get out of the arm lock you have on them, and you cannot therefore trust their information. They may well be withholding vital information as revenge. They may even betray their case officer in the hope of being forgiven by their authorities. But inducements can also be coercive. If you know a potential agent you hope to recruit has a critically ill child and you offer to provide world class medical treatment in New York then, ethically, you leave them little choice but to agree to help you. Here strategic patience is needed. An offer to help their family, once they have volunteered their services, will on the other hand ensure their lasting gratitude and cooperation.

———◊◊◊◊◊◊◊———

In the later stages of the Cold War the pendulum had therefore swung, and it was then Soviet and Warsaw Pact citizens, including disillusioned officers in their intelligence services who were volunteering for ideological reasons to work for CIA and MI6 to help bring down the communist regimes. There are several examples of such ideological agents working from the inside to help destroy the KGB. The KGB archivist Vassili Mitrokhin spent years making notes on KGB operational cases before defecting with his trove of information to MI6.[11] More recently Colonel Gordievsky rose inside the KGB while an active MI6 agent to become acting head of the KGB residency in the Soviet Embassy.[12]

The ethical duty of care lasts beyond the actual period of service of an agent in place which can be problematic. Perhaps the most important Western counterintelligence agent of the Cold War was Mikhael Goleniewski who was the deputy head of Czech counterintelligence, while also working as the KGB's undercover man in Prague. He knew of penetrations in all the NATO nations and in the CIA and decided to help the FBI to catch them. So he asked a U.S. diplomat in Prague to pass his offer of service to J. Edgar Hoover at the FBI. But the diplomat instead simply passed the letter to the CIA head of station, who then ran Goleniewski pretending to be an FBI officer for some years as that most valuable of assets, an agent in place. The CIA shared some of his hugely valuable intelligence with MI6 in London, where sadly it passed over the desk of George Blake, himself a KGB agent, who promptly told Moscow they had a leak. Goleniewski panicked and ran—you can imagine his loss of confidence when he discovered he had all along been deceptively run by the CIA, not the FBI, and that as he had feared at the outset, the CIA had inadvertently put his life in danger. Ego and a love of excitement itself (he turned out to be a bigamist) seems to have played a big part in his thinking that he could get away with such a complex life. Sadly, his grip on reality after his defection and resettlement in the United States began to falter, and he ended by going public with the embarrassing and wholly false claim he was the last of the Romanovs and rightful heir to the murdered Russian czar's fortune.[13] Aftercare of burned-out agents is a heavy ethical responsibility.

In conclusion, the famous categorical imperative of the most famous moral philosopher of all, Immanuel Kant, demands that we act only according to the maxim that at the same time our act should be regarded as a universal law. If we permit torture then we can hardly complain that it is wrong when others do it to us. For Kant, rational human beings should be treated as an end in themselves and not as a means to something else. The fact that we are human has value in itself and people cannot just be used as means to our intelligence ends.

But stealing secrets is what intelligence officers have to do, knowing therefore they will fall short of Kant's categorical imperative. They will at times have to manipulate and deceive people. They will have to encourage agents to take risks to help us, inevitably treating them as a means to the end of gathering intelligence. But ethical principles can nevertheless govern the risks an agent is asked to run, and the risks to their families, and the risks they may face when they retire.

What I hope distinguishes our intelligence activity from the same techniques used in the service of totalitarian regimes is in the ethical values that our intelligence activity seeks to defend and must, therefore, embody. The novelist John le Carré gave his answer, as a former British intelligence officer himself, to defend his spying, "It was justifiable to betray the trust of people whom you have befriended in order to gain information for the British state, as it helped to defend a free society."[14]

To conclude, in his memoirs former U.S. director of central intelligence Adm. Stansfield Turner wrote that "there is one overall test of the ethics of human intelligence activities. That is whether those approving them feel they could defend their decisions before the public—if the actions became public."[15]

That is the basis of the advice I have always given as a British public servant to senior ministers. However, the admiral was clear about what he was *not* saying. His guideline does not say only authorize actions if you think the public would approve of them if they knew of them. Rather, it says be so convinced of the importance of the action that you would accept any criticism that might develop if the covert actions did become public, and that you know you could therefore construct a convincing defense of the ethics of the decision as being necessary in the circumstance and proportionate in its methods.

NOTES

1. See the many examples in Christopher Andrew, *The Secret World: A History of Intelligence* (London: Allen Lane, 2018).
2. Old Testament, *Book of Joshua*, vol. 2.
3. David Omand and Mark Phythian, *Principled Spying* (Oxford: Oxford University Press, 2018).
4. Michael Waltzer, *Just and Unjust Wars: A Moral Argument with Historical Illustrations* (Harmonsworth: Penguin Books, 1980).
5. Michael Quinlan, "Just intelligence: prolegomena to an ethical theory," *Intelligence and National Security* 22, no. 1 (2007): 1–13.
6. An example is the July 2021 exposure of the widespread use of Pegasus malware sold by an Israeli security company NSO to more than forty governments around the world; see David Kaye and Marietje Schaake, "Global spyware such as Pegasus is a threat to democracy," *Washington Post Opinion*, July 19, 2021, https://www.washingtonpost.com/opinions/2021/07/19/pegasus-spyware-nso-group-threat-democracy-journalism/, accessed July 23, 2021.
7. Peter Taylor, *Brits: The War against the IRA* (London: Bloomsbury, 2001), 295.
8. "Video re-emerges of Putin threat that 'traitors will kick the bucket.'" https://www.independent.co.uk/news/world/europe/vladimir-putin-traitors-kick-bucket-sergei-skripal-latest-video-30-pieces-silver-a8243206.html, accessed July 17, 2021.
9. British Government, *Consolidated Guidance to Intelligence Officers and Service Personnel on the Detention and Interviewing of Detainees Overseas*. London: HMSO, July 2010, https://assets.publishing.service.gov.uk/government/uploads/system/uploads/attachment_data/file/62632/Consolidated_Guidance_November_2011.pdf

10. Michael J. Sulick, *American Spies* (Washington, DC: Georgetown University Press, 2013).

11. Christopher Andrew and Vasili Mitrokhin, *The Mitrokhin Archive Volume 1, The KGB in Europe and the West* (London: Allen Lane, 1999). Christopher Andrew and Vasili Mitrokhin, *The Mitrokhin Archive Volume 2, The KGB and the World* (London: Allen Lane, 2005).

12. A highly readable and accurate account of the case is Ben Macintyre, *The Spy and the Traitor* (London: Penguin Books, 2018).

13. Tim Tate, *The Spy Who Was Left Out in the Cold* (London: Transworld Publishers, 2021).

14. Adam Sisman, *John Le Carré: The Biography* (London: Bloomsbury, 2015), 543. In an interview for BBC television at around this time, Cornwell said that spying "felt like betrayal, but it had a voluptuous quality: this was a necessary sacrifice of morality and that is a very important component of what makes people spy, what attracts them."

15. Stansfield Turner, *Secrecy and Democracy: The CIA in Transition* (New York: Houghton Mifflin, 1985).

7 | Secrecy, Deception, and Covert Action
Mitt Regan

This chapter considers whether, as an ethical matter, a state must take responsibility for operations that it has conducted or supported in another state to affect events in that state. That is, apart from any ethical issues that may arise because of the nature of the operations, does a decision to conduct them covertly rather than overtly raise any ethical issues?

The U.S. covert action statute defines covert action as "an activity or activities of the United States Government to influence political, economic, or military conditions abroad, where it is intended that the role of the United States Government will not be apparent or acknowledged publicly."[1] A state does this when it denies responsibility, or simply remains silent in the face of claims that it is responsible for activities in another state. Covert action consists of several types of operations, traditionally characterized in terms of the broad categories of information and psychological operations, political action, security and military assistance, and direct action.

Information operations seek to influence the beliefs of a target audience. Such operations may take different forms and have different objectives. One type of campaign is meant to discredit an adversary by dissemination of information that casts the adversary in a bad light, while avoiding attribution of the dissemination to the state circulating it. Thus, State A may circulate, or help State B government opponents circulate, claims that State B is engaging in human rights violations, or that State B public officials are corruptly using public funds for their own advantage. Or it may circulate or help the government circulate information designed to discredit government opponents.

Political action consists of various measures, often in combination, intended to strengthen the political position of either a friendly government or opponents of an unfriendly one. Because of the desire to affect the perception of the amount of domestic political support for one side or the other, such operations take the form of covert state assistance to a regime or to local groups that conceals the fact that a foreign state is involved. Activities may involve information operations, but also can include funding to help establish local organizations, mobilize supporters, and organize demonstrations.

A state also may provide military assistance to the government or its opponents. Such assistance may consist of providing funds, logistical support, intelligence, arms, and/or training to forces in another state. The purpose may be to enhance the government's ability to engage in law enforcement operations, foreign internal defense, hostilities with another state, or a conflict with insurgents. Or a state may provide assistance to government opponents. Such assistance may occur in combination with information operations and political action, but represents an intensification of support in that the resources it provides can be used for violent purposes by the recipient group. Finally, direct action consists of operations to detain individuals or use force against them, including missions to rescue nationals abroad.

Each of these operations has been the focus of several analyses that address whether and how they may be justified or excused. Thus, for instance, covert information operations may raise issues with respect to disseminating false information, political action may involve questions about interference with foreign state sovereignty and political processes, and the provision of weapons and training to government or insurgent forces may require assessing ethical concerns relating to taking sides in an internal political conflict in another state, as well as possible issues regarding furnishing assistance to others that enables them to use force.

Even if an overt operation is ethical based on analysis of its substantive effects, does conducting it covertly require an additional ethical justification in order to conduct it covertly? Should there be at least a presumption that a state should take responsibility for efforts to influence events in other states? If so, even activities that are justified if done overtly require separate justification for being conducted covertly. While there appears to be an intuition that acting covertly is not entirely reputable, there has been surprisingly little attention to whether this intuition has any ethical basis. This chapter seeks to explore whether it does.

RURITANIAN COVERT ACTION IN ARCADIA

Imagine the following scenario: You are citizen of Arcadia, a state that has a parliamentary form of government. The current prime minister (PM) is head of a coalition government that has been in power for a few years and is generally popular. However, a small segment of the population, who call themselves "True Folk," is bitterly opposed to the PM and the administration. Members criticize the administration on a handful of social media sites, as well as in online publications that are known to be sponsored by their members.

True Folk also runs some commercials on television and radio, and some advertisements online. These reach wider audiences, but the opponents can't afford to do them very often. Members also regularly write their members of parliament, but they constitute a small percentage of voters and so have not had much influence. Attacks on the PM do not affect the ability of the administration to carry out its responsibilities, but administration spokespersons periodically take time to challenge claims by the opposition that they regard as especially inaccurate or misleading.

Over the course of a few months, there seems to be a significant increase in opposition to the administration. A larger number of individuals and groups that do not appear affiliated with True Folk begin criticizing the administration on social media. In addition, there is a dramatic increase in the number of radio and television commercials and online advertisements opposing the administration sponsored by a variety of groups. Members of parliament report receiving an increasing volume of messages that are critical of the PM, demanding that members not cooperate with him. Other messages urge parties that are part of the governing coalition to withdraw from it and declare that they no longer have confidence in the government, which would require the PM to call an election. Demonstrations against the administration also begin to occur in several locations. When administration spokespersons respond to some of the opposition claims, there are immediate critical messages on a variety of media platforms.

This escalation of opposition leads an increasing number of journalists and political observers to suggest that the government is rapidly losing the confidence of the population. Demonstrations increase, the wave of criticism seems more widespread, and the clamor for a new election grows louder. The administration must spend a growing amount of time responding to allegations. Leaders of parties that are part of the coalition begin discussing the possibility of withdrawing their support and declaring that they have no confidence in the government. Over the course of a few months, the PM has gone from being reasonably popular to facing what political commentators now call a crisis that threatens his ability to govern and to remain in office.

Suppose that an investigation by a consortium of news agencies reveals that a few months ago another state, Ruritania, began to pour large amounts of money into supporting what at the time was a small number of administration opponents. These resources have enabled the opposition to amplify their criticism and foster the appearance of a widespread movement by establishing what appear to be independent news sources, purchasing time for commercials, placing advertisements in a large number of publications, generating multiple messages to members of parliament that appear to be from people in their districts, and hiring people to organize demonstrations against the administration. All these activities have enabled True Folk to conduct a massive campaign that has changed public attitudes. Despite this evidence, Ruritania denies that it has provided any assistance to True Folk.

Ruritania has engaged in covert political action, carried out in part through information operations. Its goal may be to undermine a government that Ruritania regards as unfriendly, but it also may be simply to create instability and discord in Arcadia that hampers the ability of the government to act.

Are you concerned when you learn about what Ruritania has done? Specifically, aside from the particular activities that Ruritania has conducted, has it acted wrongly because it has conducted these activities without anyone knowing that it is involved? While covert action that has certain severe effects may be unlawful under international law, acting covertly in itself is not. Regardless of the law, however, is acting covertly unethical? What analytical framework can we use to answer this question?

SECRECY AND DECEPTION

A useful place to begin ethical analysis is to ask who might be wronged if a state acts covertly. We could think of acting covertly as simply engaging in secrecy: keeping secret the identity of the responsible state. If this is the case, acting secretly may not be wrongful. As Sissela Bok has noted, we accept that some measure of secrecy in life is appropriate and desirable. As she says, "Whereas I take lying to be prima facie wrong, with a negative presumption against it from the outset, secrecy need not be. Whereas every lie stands in need of justification, all secrets do not."[2]

This appears to be true in relations among states, since it is common for states to keep secrets from one another. While scholars have described the potential benefits of transparency in international politics, "[i]f transparency is so valuable, why are many records, proceedings, and outcomes kept hidden from domestic publics, other states, and market actors?"[3] As Allison Carnegie has noted, "Secret actions could include, for example, propaganda, political operations, economic actions, and paramilitary actions, while secret information could include covert agreements signed between states or the secretive monitoring of those agreements."[4]

In the realm of relations among states, with some limiting conditions, we generally can look to state practice to determine states' expectations with regard to each other. These expectations reflect their understanding of their rights and obligations to one another, and thus what they consider ethical and unethical behavior. Absent agreement or special circumstances, states appear to believe that it is not unethical to keep secrets from one another. If acting covertly simply involves acting secretly, it therefore does not appear ethically problematic.

In some cases, however, a secret may be what Dennis Thompson and Amy Guttman call a "deceptive secret." As they describe it, "An official who conceals information with the intention of causing [people] to believe something the official knows is false creates a deceptive secret."[5] Keeping secret the identity of a state responsible for an operation arguably involves not only secrecy but deception. It is meant to mislead both those affected by an operation and the larger public to believe that a state is not responsible for the operation it has conducted, and perhaps even to attribute it to another actor.

A state's failure to acknowledge responsibility is meant to create the false impression that it played no role in bringing about the events in question. I regard this as the case regardless of whether a state explicitly denies responsibility, or simply fails to admit it. When this occurs, a state engages in what I call "attribution deception." With respect to deception, as compared to secrecy, there is a stronger consensus in ordinary life that it is wrong, even if it may be justified in some circumstances. Is this also true about attribution deception by states?

Engaging in deception involves keeping information from a party to which they are entitled. The first step in analyzing whether acting covertly is ethical therefore is determining who, if anyone, has a right to know the identity of a state that is conducting activities in another state. Attribution deception is depriving such a party of this information. This constitutes a presumptive wrong, which must be rebutted by an adequate justification in order to avoid being ethically blameworthy. The obligation to provide a justification would not be legally enforceable, but the failure to do so would subject a state to criticism. This in turn might result in hostile behavior by the party that believes that it has been wronged, with the support of the international community. This would reflect enforcement of norms, not legal enforcement.

Does acting covertly violate a presumptive right of states to know when other states are involved in various activities abroad? Are states in general entitled to this information so that they can make informed decisions? Even if not, might a state in which covert action occurs be entitled to it? In addition, do residents of a state in which another state acts covertly have an entitlement to this information independent of any entitlement that their own state may have? Or are states the only parties in the international order who have rights and obligations?

The next section analyzes these questions with respect to the covert action by Ruritania in Arcadia described previously. It considers the threshold question of when there may be a plausible claim that a party has been wronged by attribution deception. A full ethical analysis would require a determination of what kinds of justifications would be sufficient to avoid a claim that acting covertly is wrongful. I do not attempt such analysis in this paper. My goal is the more modest one of attempting to advance our thinking about the ethics of acting covertly by clarifying when it may be presumptively wrong.

I argue that whether attribution deception is unethical cannot be determined with respect to covert action in general, but requires close analysis of the specific interests affected by particular types of covert operations. Different parties may have entitlements depending on the operation in question.

Before beginning this analysis, it is worth considering a threshold practical objection. My analytical framework suggests that some parties may plausibly claim to be wronged by different types of operations that are conducted covertly rather than overtly, but that others may not. To the extent that I conclude that this establishes a presumption in favor of acting overtly that is not rebutted by other considerations, the result may be that a state may have an ethical responsibility to acknowledge its involvement to some audiences but not others. As a practical matter, however, this may be infeasible, since it is difficult to confine public attribution to certain discrete audiences. One therefore may claim that as long as at least one group is entitled to information about attribution, a state no longer can ethically conduct certain types of operations covertly at all.

This is a fair point, but I believe that there are two reasons that it nonetheless is worth identifying those parties who may and may not be wronged by a state acting covertly. First, such analysis can clarify what kinds of interests are at stake, and the magnitude of those interests, in choosing to conduct an operation covertly. Making such distinctions should contribute to the rigor and depth of ethical analysis of this choice, by helping clarify the full consequences of a decision to act covertly.

Second, it may be possible in at least some cases to disclose the identity of the state involved in a covert operation to some parties but not others. Clarity about who will be wronged by acting covertly can guide this decision. Finally, when disclosure to one group entitled to information unavoidably means disclosure to another group who is not, the weight of the first group's interest and the risk of disclosure to the second could lead to an all-things-considered judgment that an operation can be conducted covertly. In order to arrive at such a judgment, we need as refined an analysis as possible of the possible wrongs and risks from proceeding covertly.

RURITANIAN COVERT ASSISTANCE TO GOVERNMENT OPPONENTS

Which, if any, parties might be wronged by Ruritania not acknowledging that it has provided assistance to opponents of the government in Arcadia? First, are the citizens of *Ruritania* wronged? Are they entitled to know when their government attempts to influence the political process in another state? The liberal democratic principle of self-determination provides a powerful basis for this claim, on the ground that attribution deception citizens of information they need to hold their government accountable.

We might look to Kant's principle of publicity as an expression of this idea. That principle essentially says that an action is wrong if the state cannot publicly justify it. As David Luban has said, a decision maker must ask, "Could I still get away with this if the fact that I am doing it were publicly known?"[6] One might argue that a state that believes that it can only act if it does so covertly violates this principle.

If we think of that principle, however, as applicable to general rules and policies rather than specific decisions, a state might act consistently with it if it informs the public that it may be necessary in some cases to act covertly. As Luban puts it, "If the reasons for keeping a first-order policy secret can themselves be justified in a public manner, then the second-order policy of keeping the first-order policy secret is fully compatible with the publicity principle."[7]

What is crucial, however, is that there maybe some mechanism for meaningful democratic oversight so that officials can be held accountable, such as disclosure to a legislative committee. By doing so, a state honors the principle of democratic self-determination that is the foundation of the publicity principle. Democratically accountable representatives are aware of the role of the state in an operation and are in a position to challenge or otherwise influence that operation based on their judgment of its benefits and risks. Citizens of a state that acts covertly thus have a claim that they are entitled to know when their government acts covertly, but adequate oversight by democratically accountable representatives can satisfy their claim.

Any claim of entitlement by parties outside Ruritania must be based on an argument different from the self-determination claim available to citizens of Ruritania. What about the state of Arcadia? Is it entitled to know that Ruritania has enabled government opponents to substantially increase their influence within Arcadia? Arcadia may argue that it has an ethical responsibility to perform its sovereign functions in the name of and for the benefit of its citizens. Its ability to perform these functions requires that it have an informed understanding of the wishes of its citizens. Information that another state is providing assistance to an opposition group is important to the government in gaining an accurate assessment of the depth and breadth of domestic political sentiment. The government needs to know how much this sentiment reflects genuine indigenous views, and how much it reflects foreign state influence?

The government can argue that both sides should have information about the extent to which views that are expressed in domestic political debate may be influenced by the interests of another state. Pointing out the possibility of such influence is a legitimate strategy by both sides in the political conflict that enable citizens to make more fully informed decisions. If the Arcadian government is unaware that Ruritania is providing assistance to its opponents, this will prevent the government from effectively defending itself by publicly identifying and criticizing Ruritania's motives for doing so. Arcadia thus may claim that Ruritania has wronged it by acting covertly. This means that Arcadia can publicly claim that Ruritania has acted unethically unless Ruritania can provide a justification for acting covertly.

Should Arcadian citizens not involved in opposing the government be entitled to know that opponents are receiving assistance from Ruritania that enhances their ability to engage in political action? Or do only states have entitlements in the international arena? States traditionally have been regarded as the only parties that have rights and obligations to one another under international law. The assumption has been that citizens' rights are derived from those of the states in which they reside. Citizens presumptively can rely on states to protect their interests, and therefore need not be regarded as independent rights holders.

This view may have been plausible when sovereignty was regarded as an inviolable principle, and the interests of individuals were seen as derived from the interests of the states of which they are members. In the last several decades, however, there has been increasing commitment to the idea that individuals have rights based on their intrinsic dignity and worth, rather than solely on their membership in particular political communities. This in turn has made sovereignty more qualified, contingent on at least minimal state respect for the human rights of their populations.

The result is that it is possible to imagine that the interests and rights of states and of individuals within them are not completely coterminous. If this is so, we cannot automatically assume that states will act as agents that fully protect the human rights of their subjects when they interact with one another. We may presume that this is the case in states that we regard as respectful of their citizens' human rights. This presumption is open to rebuttal, however, depending on particular circumstances, and the discussion next suggests one instance in which the interests of a state and its citizens may diverge. In sum, we must consider whether attribution deception deprives individuals, not simply states, of information to which they are entitled. Even if each may have a claim, the basis for that claim may differ between them.

Arcadian citizens may claim that attribution deception by Ruritania in this case violates their right to self-determination, in that it deprives them of information they need to make an informed decision about their shared political life. Knowledge that Ruritania is providing assistance to opponents of the Arcadia government is valuable for self-determination because it enhances Arcadian citizens' ability to accurately determine the level of opposition to the government. It enables them to consider to what extent opposition reflects fellow citizens' dissatisfaction with the government, and how much it reflects the influence of Ruritania's interests. This is relevant in evaluating whether opposition success would result in a government that is beholden in some way to Ruritania. Citizens therefore may have a plausible claim that they are wronged by Ruritania's failure to acknowledge its assistance to government opponents.

What about other states? Do they have a right to know the identity of Ruritania? Unlike Arcadia, they have no claim based on sovereignty. Nor, unlike citizens of Arcadia, do they have a claim based on self-determination. I have already suggested that states as a general matter are not wronged by attribution deception. Transparency about who is supporting whom in the international arena may be an aspiration, but it does not as yet constitute a norm whose violation wrongs other states. The creation of secret alliances is a practice in which many states participate, and in which they appear to acquiesce.

The limits of state tolerance are reflected in international law. States may lawfully engage in a wide variety of activities that seek to gain advantage at the expense of one another. International law, however, provides that they may not go so far as to engage in behavior that constitutes "intervention" interfering with another state's exercise of sovereign functions. The 1970 United Nations General Assembly Declaration on the Inadmissibility of Intervention in the Domestic Affairs of States and the Protection of Their Independence and Sovereignty provides, "Every State has an inalienable right to choose its political, economic, social and cultural systems, without interference in any form by another State."[8] The International Court of Justice in *Nicaragua v. United States* affirmed this as a principle of customary international law, stating, "A prohibited intervention must . . . be one bearing on matters in which each State is permitted, by the principle of State sovereignty, to decide freely. . . . Intervention is wrongful when it uses methods of coercion in regard to such choices, which must remain free ones."[9]

Whether states other than Arcadia are wronged by Ruritania acting covertly in this case therefore should depend on whether Ruritanian operations constitute unlawful intervention. If it does, other states have a claim that they are wronged. International law, particularly customary international law, operates through the actions of states in response to one another. States therefore are entitled to know when a violation of international law occurs because one state's assistance to another has undermined the latter's ability to act as an independent sovereign. The viability of the norm against intervention depends upon the expression of state disapproval of such conduct. Attribution deception in the course of an unlawful intervention thus prevents the international community of nontargeted states from being able to sustain at least a minimally cooperative international order.

Not only individual states, but the system of international law in general, therefore suffers a wrong when states act covertly in order to conceal violation of a norm. There may, of course, be disagreement about whether a violation has occurred, but debate on this question itself helps to refine and clarify the contours of international law. This suggests that there need not be a complete consensus on the existence of a violation in order to trigger this entitlement, although I will not attempt here to specify what threshold should suffice.

In sum, Arcadia arguably has a claim that it has been wronged by Ruritania covertly providing assistance to opponents of the government of Arcadia because being deprived of this information impairs its ability to govern effectively based on an accurate understanding of its citizens' views and desires. This claim is grounded in sovereignty, although it does not depend on such impairment being so substantial that it constitutes unlawful intervention.

Arcadian citizens have an independent claim that attribution deception prevents them from effectively engaging in self-determination. Other states are wronged by attribution deception in this case only if it violates the prohibition on unlawful intervention. Short of that, they have no claim that Ruritania has deprived them of information to which they are entitled.

How might individuals be wronged by attribution deception when their state is not? The next section discusses this possibility.

RURITANIA COVERT ASSISTANCE TO THE GOVERNMENT

Suppose that Ruritania covertly provides military assistance to Arcadia. The Arcadian government obviously is aware of this assistance. Are its citizens entitled to know about it? There is an argument that they are because knowledge of Ruritanian support enables them to monitor possible foreign influence on the government's decisions. Arcadian citizens are entitled to know of this possibility so that they can hold their government accountable for serving the best interests of Arcadia, and not those of a foreign state.

Do other states have a claim of entitlement to such information? Based on the analysis of political action discussed earlier, they arguably do not, unless Ruritanian assistance violates international law.

What if Arcadia asks Ruritania not to disclose the assistance? Would Ruritania be justified in acting covertly based on this request? Arcadia may believe that receiving Ruritanian support is in the best interest of its citizens because it enhances Arcadia's ability to defend them. It may also believe, however, that a portion of its citizens are unreasonably hostile to Ruritania and that their objection might imperil the ability to receive this assistance. In addition, Arcadia may be concerned that states in its region would disapprove of such assistance. The government claims that these are legitimate concerns that may be taken into account in exercising its sovereignty. That is, the government has the right and the obligation to exercise sovereignty in the manner that it believes best serves its citizens.

Should Ruritania honor Arcadia's request to conceal its military support? On the one hand, we might say that Ruritania effectively is helping Arcadia violate the publicity principle with respect to Arcadian citizens. As such, it is abetting Arcadia's interference with its own citizens' right of self-determination.

On the other hand, would Ruritania's refusal to honor the government's request interfere with Arcadia's sovereign right to govern as it sees fit? This is a fundamental norm of the international order—that states have no right to intrude on the exercise of sovereign judgment by another state. Indeed, as I have described, this norm is the basis for the prohibition of intervention. Should Ruritania determine whether its judgment about what is in the best interest of Arcadian citizens is superior to the judgment of the Arcadian government?

I think that the answer depends on the nature of the Arcadian regime. In the last few decades, the right of sovereignty has come to be regarded as contingent on minimum basic respect for the human rights of citizens. We, thus, might say that respect for sovereignty establishes a rebuttable presumption that Ruritania should honor Arcadia's request. An Arcadian record of perpetration of egregious human rights violations, however, would suffice to rebut this presumption.

Ruritania therefore will need to consider whether Arcadia's request is part of a larger pattern of serious human rights violations against its citizens, and whether this would be furthered by withholding this information from the population. If so, Ruritania need not accede to Arcadia's request. If not, respect for Arcadian sovereignty requires that it do so. This analysis does not resolve the issue of whether Arcadia is justified in concealing the identity of Ruritania from its citizens. The logic of my earlier analysis of the publicity principle, however, suggests that this may be defensible if there is meaningful legislative oversight of Arcadia's receipt of covert assistance.

CONCLUSION

This chapter is an effort to begin establishing a framework to analyze whether a decision to conduct an operation covertly—to engage in attribution deception—raises ethical issues apart from those related to the character of the operation itself. I have suggested that analysis should begin with asking who if anyone is entitled to know the identity of a state that is undertaking operations in another state. The answer to this question must be based on an assessment of the nature of operations in particular cases, rather than as a general matter. Any party with such an entitlement is presumptively wronged by attribution deception.

This presumption means that the state that is acting covertly must have an acceptable justification for not honoring a party's entitlement. A full analysis of the ethics of acting covertly, which this chapter does not undertake, must consider what types of justifications may suffice to rebut this presumption. The aim of this chapter is the more modest one of suggesting the first step in the complex analysis that is necessary to determine whether a state acts unethically when it acts covertly.

NOTES

1. 10 USC §3093(e) (2021).
2. Sissela Bok, *Secrets: On the Ethics of Concealment and Revelation* (Vintage, 1989), Kindle Location 150.
3. Allison Carnegie, "Secrecy in International Relations and Foreign Policy," *Annuaul Review of Political Sci*ience 24 (2021): 213–33.
4. Carnegie, "Secrecy in International Relations and Foreign Policy," 215.
5. Dennis Thompson and Amy Gutmann, *Democracy and Disagreement* (Harvard University Press, 1998), Kindle Location 1612.
6. David Luban, "The Publicity Principle," in *The Theory of Institutional Design*, Robert Goodin, ed. (Cambridge University Press,1998), 154–198.
7. Luban, "The Publicity Principle," 189.

8. UN General Assembly Resolution A/RES/20/2131, Declaration on the Inadmissibility of Intervention in the Domestic Affairs of States and the Protection of Their Independence and Sovereignty, December 21, 1965.

9. Case Concerning Military and Paramilitary Activities in and Against Nicaragua (*Nicaragua v. United States of America*) International Court of Justice, 1986 I.C.J. 14.

8 | *Jus Ad Vim* and Measures Short of War
Helen Frowe

INTRODUCTION

In recent years, several writers have argued that we need to develop principles of *jus ad vim* (roughly, "the right to use force") for evaluating the use of force in situations that both fall short of war and lie outside the scope of domestic law enforcement.[1] Such uses of force include, for example, isolated drone strikes and targeted assassinations. Proponents of *jus ad vim* argue that these uses of force cannot be adequately evaluated using either the familiar *jus ad bellum* principles or the principles that govern domestic policing. Here, I canvass some of the ways in which *jus ad vim* principles are said to differ from *jus ad bellum* principles. I find that the proposed *ad vim* principles add nothing to our moral reasoning and that there is no reason for those who believe that there are distinctive moral principles for evaluating war to endorse the *jus ad vim* project.

THE MORAL GAP

The *jus ad vim* project is motivated by the idea that there currently exists a moral gap in our principles for evaluating uses of force. Some uses of force occur during war and can be evaluated using familiar "just war" principles.

Others occur as part of domestic law enforcement and can be evaluated using some different set of principles (perhaps grounded in a social contract theory about the relationship between a government and the state's inhabitants). But there are some uses of force, such as isolated foreign drone strikes and assassinations, that are neither part of a broader war nor part of domestic law enforcement. According to proponents of *jus ad vim*, neither the *ad bellum* principles nor the principles that apply to domestic law enforcement are suited to evaluating these uses of force. The proposed principles of *jus ad vim* are intended to fill this gap. Notice that theirs is not a legal proposal: The claim is not that there is a gap in existing legislation that ought to be remedied. Rather, it is a moral proposal that seeks to identify distinctive moral principles for judging force short of war.

I expect that most readers will be familiar with the standard list of *ad bellum* principles: that those resorting to or waging war must have a just cause, use only force proportionate to that just cause, fight only if it is the least harmful means of achieving the just cause, and have a reasonable prospect of success by legitimate means. On some views, there is also a requirement of legitimate authority, which holds that only those with certain representative or institutional roles are permitted to wage to war. Of course, there is significant debate about what each of these principles amounts to and some are contested. But we can set those debates aside here.

How do the *ad vim* principles differ to the principles of *jus ad bellum*? Daniel Brunstetter and Megan Braun suggest that whereas the *ad bellum* principles apply only at the beginning of a war, *ad vim* principles apply throughout the use of force.[2] They also argue that *ad vim* proportionality works differently to *ad bellum* proportionality, permitting the use of force in defence of a broader range of goods.[3] Relatedly, they argue that *ad vim* employs a looser definition of just cause, and thus permits agents to forcefully pursue a broader range of ends than *jus ad bellum*.[4] But, they argue, *ad vim* proportionality is simultaneously more restrictive than *jus ad bellum*. This is partly because it sanctions only measures short of war, and partly because it pays attention not only to "the loss of civilian life but also the more subtle harms including property destruction, post-traumatic stress disorder, and social disruption."[5] Finally, they argue that *jus ad vim* includes a novel principle enjoining agents to pay attention to the prospect of escalation—that is, to the risk that using force might cause further hostilities.[6]

THEORETICAL APPROACHES TO THE MORALITY OF WAR

Do we need *jus ad vim*? That depends on the correct underlying view of the morality of war. We can divide approaches to the morality of war into two camps. The first holds that there are distinctive moral principles for evaluating war, unlike those for evaluating force in other areas of life (this is often described as the exceptionalist view).[7] The second holds that there is a single set of moral principles that applies to all spheres of life (often described as the reductivist view).[8]

It should be clear why reductivists have no need for principles of *jus ad vim*. The moral gap that *jus ad vim* is supposed to fill does not arise on the reductivist view: There are no moral gaps on this view since it holds that all our actions are subject to the same moral principles. This means that the same moral principles apply to force used during war, forceful measures short of war, forceful policing, interpersonal harming, and so on. It is only exceptionalists, who claim a distinctive set of moral principles for evaluating war, who might be attracted to the idea that there are also distinctive principles for measures short of war. After all, once we grant that morality is fragmented in the way that the exceptionalist view supposes, it is not obvious that it must fragment along the lines of "war" and "everything else."

Do exceptionalists need *jus ad vim*? That is, are the *ad bellum* principles unable to evaluate measures short of war in a way that is problematic for the exceptionalist view? Exceptionalists might offer various responses to the *ad vim* project. They might grant the picture that *ad vim* proponents assume, agreeing that there is war, measures short of war, and then not war. (Presumably "not war" can be further divided. People attracted to this view of morality might believe that, for example, the principles that govern the use of force by police officers are different from those governing harming between private citizens.)

Alternatively, exceptionalists could reject that picture, insisting that there are only two moral categories: war and not war. They might argue that the conditions that make war exceptional, and give rise to exceptional moral principles, do not arise in the conditions in which one might use measures short of war. On this view, if, for example, an isolated drone strike is not war and is prohibited by whatever the not-war principles are, then the drone strike is impermissible.

A third option is for exceptionalists to broaden their understanding of war to include the measures short of war with which *ad vim* proponents are concerned. Of course, for that to be a persuasive solution, they would also need to show that the *ad bellum* principles can be used to evaluate such uses of force. I suspect that these principles can indeed evaluate such uses of force. As I argue next, defences of *jus ad vim* largely rest on mistaken understandings of traditional just war principles. To be clear: my goal here is not to offer reductivist grounds for rejecting the *ad vim* project. Reductivism is straightforwardly incompatible with the *ad vim* project, as we saw earlier. If there are distinctive *ad vim* principles, then reductivism is false. If reductivism is true, there are no distinctive *ad vim* principles.[9] Rather, my claim is that exceptionalists have good internal reasons for rejecting the *ad vim* project, since they have good reason to reject the claim that *ad bellum* principles cannot adequately evaluate measures short of war.

THE *AD VIM* PRINCIPLES[10]
The Scope of Jus Ad Bellum

To see why exceptionalists should be sceptical of the *ad vim* project, recall the claims that I outlined previously concerning how the *jus ad vim* and *jus ad bellum* principles are supposed to differ. The first claim is that the *ad bellum* principles matter only at the outset of a war, whereas the *ad vim* principles matter throughout the use of force. As Braun and Brunstetter put it, "Whereas in war principles such as just cause and last resort need only be satisfied at the outset of a conflict, *jus ad vim* requires that they be continually reassessed in advance of each use of force."[11] The just war tradition, they say, "lacks the conceptual tools to consider the morality of an intervention that was permissible when it was launched, but that later becomes morally problematic."[12]

This is a mistaken view of when *ad bellum* principles apply. *Ad bellum* principles apply across the duration of a war. We can see this by thinking about some of the circumstances in which it would be impermissible to continue to fight. The most obvious example is securing the just cause: one may not continue to fight if one is no longer pursuing a just cause; hence, continuing to fight can be prohibited by *ad bellum* considerations. Another example is realizing that one no longer has a reasonable prospect of success. There are lots of ways in which a war that has a reasonable prospect of success at its outset might cease to have such a prospect once it is underway. For example, a belligerent might discover information about the enemy's capabilities that was unavailable at the outset of the war, or suffer a catastrophic loss that makes the chances of victory vanishingly small. It is impermissible to continue the war under these circumstances, in light of the *ad bellum* constraints. It is also impermissible to fight if war is no longer the least harmful means of securing the just cause—for example, if reasonable peace terms are offered that will secure the just cause. Here, too, it is the *ad bellum* conditions that tell us that war is unnecessary, and thus continued force is impermissible. These reflections show that it is a mistake to think that the *ad bellum* principles apply only at the moment of resort to war. Wars must be continually assessed for their compliance with the ad *bellum* principles.

Proportionality and Just Cause

What about the idea that *ad vim* includes a more favourable proportionality calculation? The claim here is that *ad vim* is sensitive to a broad range of goods, in excess of those to which *ad bellum* proportionality is sensitive. Reflecting on the nature of proportionality calculations reveals this to be a mistake. Proportionality calculations weigh goods and harms, and the (only) relevant goods are those that can weigh against—that is, help to justify—the harms that one foresees one will impose. Imagine that an agent foresees that their action will kill someone. If, for example, displays of military prowess are not the sort of good that weighs against the harm of killing, then the fact that the agent's action will display military prowess is not going to help justify their action. If, in contrast, saving lives weighs against the harm of killing, then the fact that their action will save lives will help to justify that action. Of course, not all uses of force result in lethal harm. The imposition of these lesser harms might be justified by securing less important goods that are irrelevant to justifying killing. But that's true in war as well. Insofar as a wartime action will cause less than lethal harm, it can be proportionate to cause that harm for the sake of securing correspondingly less important goods.

Given this general structure of proportionality, it is doubtful *ad vim* proportionality calculations could allow a wider range of goods to weigh against a given harm, compared to the goods deemed relevant to justifying that harm by an *ad bellum* proportionality calculation. Either the good in question is of the sort that might help to justify the prospective harm, or it is not. If the good is so relevant, then it is relevant irrespective of whether one is considering proportionality *ad bellum* or proportionality *ad vim*. If, for example, saving lives is relevant to justifying killing in war, then it is also relevant to justifying killing via measures short of war. If the good is irrelevant, then it is irrelevant irrespective of whether one is considering proportionality *ad bellum* or proportionality *ad vim*. Likewise, if harms such as property destruction, psychological distress, and social disruption are relevant to proportionality calculations for securing goods via measures short of war, then they are relevant to proportionality calculations for securing goods via war.

The only way in which an *ad vim* proportionality calculation could permit the use of force in pursuit of a broader range of goods than an *ad bellum* proportionality calculation would be for the *ad vim* calculation to ascribe less weight to harms caused outside of war. For example, if we hold that lethal harms count for less when they are imposed outside of war, then this would explain how these harms can be justified in order to secure less important goods. But that looks implausible. A person's rights against being harmed are not weaker if they will be harmed outside of a war.

These considerations also explain why the suggestion that *jus ad vim* principles employ a looser understanding of just cause is mistaken. The rationale here is that when one is considering measures short of war, one might be justified in resorting to those measures for less important causes than one could permissibly pursue by means of war. But this is, again, just a proportionality claim: on the assumption that "war" picks out a greater quantum of force, then clearly one may employ such force only for a correspondingly more important good. And again, causes that do not warrant killing in war are not going to justify killing outside of war. The question in this case remains whether securing the good warrants imposing this harm. And again, whether one is at war is irrelevant to how we answer that question.

We also saw that its proponents claim that *ad vim* produces more restrictive proportionality verdicts because it only ever sanctions measures short of war. But this apparent difference is also the result of a standard application of proportionality. If a cause is less important, then one may cause correspondingly less harm while pursuing it. Moreover, considering cases in which one might use measures short of war to prevent grave harm shows how this claim about the scope of *jus ad vim* undermines the *ad vim* project. Imagine that a state is able to prevent a genocide via a single drone strike, taking out the entire leadership of the genocidal campaign. The single strike would be a measure short of war. Thus, it looks like a matter for *jus ad vim*—that is, it looks like a use of force that should be judged using the proposed *ad vim* principles. But this does not show that it would be disproportionate to use more force in order to prevent the genocide. If the drone strike fails, the state need not simply let the genocide occur since the *ad vim* principles restrict force to only these limited measures. On the contrary, the state may employ further, greater force if the drone strike fails, plausibly including force on a scale that counts as war.

Thinking about these cases reveals that whether the *ad vim* principles prohibit a use of force will not tell us that the use of force is in fact prohibited. Once one reaches the limits of the force that can be sanctioned by the *ad vim* principles, one simply moves to the *ad bellum* principles. But of course, once one makes this move, one would still be asking the same question: Does securing this good warrant imposing this harm? *Ad vim* proportionality adds nothing to our moral reasoning that is not contained in usual *ad bellum* proportionality calculations.

Escalation

What about the idea that *jus ad vim* contains a distinctive principle enjoining agents to be sensitive to the prospect of escalating force? This will be a distinctive principle only if the principles of *jus ad bellum* are insensitive to escalation. But *ad bellum* proportionality calculations plausibly include risks of escalation. To see this, consider the following case:

> *Land*: State A has occupied a small, unremarkable and unoccupied piece of State B's land. State B can expel A's occupying force by sending

in some tanks. Such a show of force will cause the occupying troops to withdraw. However, State A will almost certainly respond with a full-scale invasion of State B that State B will be able to repel only via a protracted war that will cause twenty thousand deaths.

The initial response of sending in some tanks might seem proportionate, taken in isolation. But clearly the proportionality requirement does not permit State B to consider that action in isolation. Rather, State B must take into account the likely escalation. Regaining control of this piece of land does not warrant 20,000 deaths. Since that will be the likely result of sending in the tanks, it is disproportionate to send in the tanks.

Theorists of defensive force disagree about exactly how we should deal with escalation cases (for example, whether such harms are discounted in proportionality calculations compared to other harms).[13] But these debates are irrelevant to whether sensitivity to escalation is a distinctive feature of *jus ad vim*. Whatever turns out to be the correct way to accommodate escalation will surely be correct with respect to both escalation within war and escalation using measures short of war. It is implausible that risks of escalation matter outside of, but not within, war.

SUMMARY

The proposed features of *jus ad vim* canvassed here do not give exceptionalists reason to embrace *jus ad vim* principles. The alleged differences between *jus ad vim* and *jus ad bellum* rest on mistaken understandings of the nature and application of the *ad bellum* principles. If exceptionalists broaden their concept of war to include a range of measures outside of conventional war, it seems plausible that they can use the familiar *ad bellum* principles to evaluate those uses of force.

NOTES

1. See Megan Braun and Daniel Brunstetter, "Rethinking the Criterion for Assessing CIA-Targeted Killings: Drones, Proportionality and *Jus Ad Vim*," *Journal of Military Ethics*, 112, no. 4 (2014): 304–24; Daniel Brunstetter and Megan Braun, "'From *Jus Ad Bellum* to *Jus Ad Vim*: Recalibrating Our Understanding of the Moral Use of Force," *Ethics and International Affairs* 27, no. 1 (2013): 87–106; Brandt S. Ford, "*Jus Ad Vim* and the Just Use of Lethal

Force-Short-of-War," in *Routledge Handbook of Ethics and War* Fritz Allhoff, Nicholas Evans, and Adam Henschke, eds. (Abingdon, U.K.: Routledge, 2013), 63–75. For a collection of essays on *jus ad vim*, see Jai Galliott, ed., *Force Short of War in Modern Conflict: Jus Ad Vim* (Edinburgh University Press, 2019).

2. Braun and Brunstetter, "Rethinking the Criterion for Assessing CIA-Targeted Killings," 317.

3. Braun and Brunstetter, "'Rethinking the Criterion for Assessing CIA-Targeted Killings," 318.

4. Brunstetter and Braun, "From *Jus Ad Bellum* to *Jus Ad Vim*," 96.

5. Braun and Brunstetter, "Rethinking the Criterion for Assessing CIA-Targeted Killings," 318–19.

6. Brunstetter and Braun, "From *Jus ad Bellum* to *Jus Ad Vim*," 99.

7. For defence of exceptionalism, see Michael Walzer, *Just and Unjust Wars: A Moral Argument with Historical Illustrations* (Basic Books, 1974); Noam Zohar, "Collective War and Individualistic Ethics: Against the Conscription of 'Self-Defense," *Political Theory* 21 no. 4 (1993): 606–22; Christopher Kutz, "The Difference Uniforms Make: Collective Violence in Criminal Law and War," *Philosophy and Public Affairs* 33 no. 2 (2005): 148–80; Seth Lazar, "Necessity in Self-Defense and War," *Philosophy and Public Affairs*, 40, no. 1 (2012): 3–44; David Rodin, *War and Self-Defence* (New York: Oxford University Press, 2002).

8. For defence of reductivism, see Jeff McMahan, *Killing in War* (Oxford: Oxford University Press, 2009); Helen Frowe, *Defensive Killing* (Oxford: Oxford University Press, 2014); Cécile Fabre, *Cosmopolitan War* (Oxford: Oxford University Press, 2011); Adil Ahmad Haque, *Law and Morality at War* (Oxford: Oxford University Press, 2017).

9. Claims that the *ad vim* project represents neutral ground between exceptionalists and reductivists are thus confused. See Christian Braun and Jai Galliott, "*Jus Ad Vim* and the Question of How to Do Just War Theory," in *Force Short of War in Modern Conflict: Jus Ad Vim* ed. Jai Galliott (Edinburgh University Press, 2019), and Daniel Brunstetter, "*Jus Ad Vim*: A Rejoinder to Helen Frowe," *Ethics and International Affairs* 30, no. 1 (2016): 131–36.

10. The arguments in this section partly draw on Helen Frowe, "On the Redundancy of *Jus Ad Vim*: A Response to Daniel Brunstetter and Megan Braun," *Ethics and International Affairs* 30, no. 1 (2016): 117–29.

11. Braun and Brunstetter, "Rethinking the Criterion for Assessing CIA-Targeted Killings," 317.

12. Brunstetter and Braun, "From *Jus Ad Bellum* to *Jus Ad Vim*," 99.

13. For discussion, see Helen Frowe, *Defensive Killing* (Oxford: Oxford University Press: 2014).

9 | An Ethical Framework for Grey Zone Responses
Edward Barrett

My comments are drawn mainly from three articles I've written. The first is a 2015 piece on the applicability of the just war tradition to military cyber operations. In the conclusion, I wrote, "[W]hile the [just war] criteria provide clear guidelines concerning lethal defensive responses to cyber-attacks, and concerning the use of cyber force within wars, they lack specificity concerning justified responses to the constant low-level harm most likely to be encountered in cyberspace." A 2017 piece took up that issue in a section uncreatively titled "Ethically Justified Responses to Sublethal Harm." And in a forthcoming article, I've developed these analyses, and applied them to five cases: the disabling of 911 emergency response systems, logic bombs in electrical grids, cybercrime and cyber espionage that shave 5 percent from our gross domestic product (GDP), electronic voting machine malware that changes the result of a presidential election, and disinformation that undermines confidence in vaccines.

Based on all this work, I offer several suggestions that together comprise a sort of unified theory of the ethics of war and grey zone operations, with an emphasis on sublethal responses within the grey zone.

First, and perhaps shockingly to midshipmen who have taken our core ethics course, the distinction between the *ad bellum* and *in bello* just war criteria should not be overdrawn. Except for legitimate authority and right intention, all the criteria are generated by the principles of rights forfeiture and double effect. Rights forfeiture is a function of narrow proportionality, effectiveness and necessity, and perhaps culpability. (Narrow proportionality means that the severity of the rights violation determines the harm permitted in response.) The forfeiture-related just war criteria are just cause, reasonable chance of success, and last resort *ad bellum*; and discrimination and necessity *in bello*. The double effect-related criteria are *ad bellum* and *in bello* proportionality. Complicating matters: just cause, reasonable chance, legitimate authority, and right intention also apply *in bello*. The categorization and naming of the criteria exist mainly in order to emphasize the moral issues most relevant at those junctures.

Second, the distinction between principles relevant to war versus the grey zone also should not be overdrawn. The principles of rights forfeiture and double effect determine permissible responses to all unjustified harm, whether or not the harm rises to the level of "cause for war." Defensive responses must be narrowly proportionate, effective, and necessary; and unavoidable side effect harm to innocents must be (widely) proportionate. Ultimately, narrow proportionality determines what type of response is justified—lethal or sublethal. When you add considerations of effectiveness, necessity, and proportionality, you get a spectrum of justified responses that range from large-scale lethal to small-scale sublethal.

Third, while most malicious cyber activities do not warrant a lethal response, some would be a cause for war. An obvious example is a cyberattack that causes the widespread destruction of electrical generators during winter (assuming that attribution is reliable). More complicated examples are logic bombs and cyber-based reductions in GDP. On logic bombs: Despite the extraordinary stakes, nothing harmful has happened yet. So unless an attack is preprogrammed and one is privy to the activation time, someone contemplating a lethal defensive response would have to satisfy the demanding requirements of preventive defense, which is morally hazardous because attaining certainty about intentions is so difficult. Similarly, even if accumulating low-level GDP reductions were part of an existentially threatening campaign, defensive uses of lethal force would be preventive, and beset with the same moral hazard.

Fourth, and in agreement with Helen Frowe, when limited lethal responses are morally appropriate (for example, interrupting 911 capabilities, or undermining confidence in vaccines), they do not require justification according to a separate *jus ad vim* framework. Although *ad vim* defenders highlight important and often forgotten issues such as escalation, the traditional criteria incorporate all the concerns allegedly addressed only by the *ad vim* framework.

Fifth, although a narrow proportionality-driven requirement to respond only sublethally might be frustrating, this limitation also opens the door to punitive harm. This assertion needs a bit of unpacking. The justified ends of harm are defense (including recovery) and punishment. Examples of punitive harm are the capital punishment of safely imprisoned criminals, austere incarceration conditions, and noncompensatory fines. Now the traditional justifications for punitive harm are retributive and consequentialist. Retributivists argue that harming wrongdoers is justified because they deserve it; their suffering is good in itself. Consequentialists justify punitive harm as an effective and necessary means to attaining rights-related benefits, namely the specific deterrence of a perpetrator from engaging in future wrongdoing, the reform of the perpetrator, and the general deterrence of other would-be wrongdoers.

Although the relative merits of these punishment justifications are still debated, I'll offer three assumptions that are restrictive and resonate in liberal societies. First, human rights and their forfeiture require that intentionally inflicted suffering serve a purpose, thus ruling out desert-based retributive punishments.[1] Second, human rights and their forfeiture require that even wrongdoers not be used as an example-setting means of preventing possible wrongful acts by unspecified others. This deontological requirement rules out the general deterrence justification. One could argue that a right to not be intentionally punished in order to deter others could be overridden by the utility of general deterrence, but I suspect that this utility would be difficult to prove or insufficient to override the right. However, general deterrence can be a side effect of permissible defensive and punitive harm.[2] Third, the remaining and legitimate consequentialist purposes of punishment are specific deterrence and reform.

Because lethal harm cannot accomplish these two purposes, capital punishment qua punishment and punitive war are impermissible. But sublethal harm can deter and reform wrongdoers, and therefore may be used both defensively and punitively if narrowly proportionate, effective, and necessary. Given that reform is unlikely when dealing with foreign aggressors, the primary purpose of such punitive harm would be specific deterrence. Accordingly, punitive measures would seek not to degrade harmful capabilities, but instead to alleviate malevolent intentions by degrading the wrongdoer's standard of living—especially personal property and reputation. And ideally, such measures would have a defensive effect and render further harms unnecessary.[3]

Sixth, a requirement to respond sublethally also opens the door to targeting those who are indirectly participating in unjustified harm. This assertion also needs unpacking. Some have argued that culpable indirect participants in unjustified lethal harm—such as civilian financiers or munitions factory workers of an aggressor state—are morally liable to lethal defensive harm.[4] (Although someone who holds this position might also argue that there are reasons for legally protecting indirect participants from targeting.) My intuitions run in the other direction, especially when the participant's role is causally distant and/or partial. Perhaps the culpable driver of an assassin is lethally targetable, but the financiers of a collective murderous enterprise are not.

However, indirect participants in unjustified lethal or sublethal attacks may be liable to defensive and punitive sublethal harms that are narrowly proportionate, effective, and necessary—a difference that comports with criminal law. Therefore, noncooperative political leaders of the territory where a wrongdoer resides, as well as civilian accomplices such as financiers, would surely be liable to some form of defensive and punitive sublethal harms. The combination of these countermeasures and punishments might be enough to reduce the harm, and even coerce states to cooperate and accomplices to desist. Returning to two cases I mentioned earlier, in most situations, ethically permissible responses to economic and electoral harms would be sublethal. But these sublethal responses could be defensive and punitive and target direct and indirect participants. These responses could also be substantial.

I'll conclude with some notes and cautions that indicate the amount of work on justified responses that remains. First, having expanded the purpose (punishment) and recipients (indirect participants) of justified harm, it would be wise to add a cautionary note that also applies to targeted killing operations. While due process might not require courts or uniforms, extraordinary care must accompany the identification and treatment of liable individuals, and appropriately transparent institutional structures must be created to ensure such care. Second, although sublethal collateral damage is preferable to lethal, it must not be ignored. Nonparticipants are not liable to any form of harm, and any collateral damage to them must therefore be widely proportionate.[5] Third, because punishments must fit crimes, we'll need more thought about narrowly proportionate punitive harm to direct and indirect participants in international contexts. Finally, the experience embedded in statutes, case law, and law enforcement should be the source of judgments about what effectively deters criminals. Ultimately, we cannot determine which punitive measures are ethically permissible without the law.

NOTES

1. Retributivism has been defended as a means of emphasizing the validity of a society's morality—a way of "planting the flag of moral truth." However, this is a consequentialist general deterrence argument, and therefore problematic from my perspective. Alternatively, retributivism has been defended as a means of securing another consequence: a victim's right to "expressively defeat" the indignity. See David Luban, "War as Punishment," *Philosophy and Public Affairs* 39, no. 4 (2012). Luban's article is a seminal and sympathetic treatment of the historical shift away from punitive war, however. While he defends retributivism, he argues that because of human psychology and the lack of an impartial third party, punitive war in practice is revengeful and unjust because it over-harms (citing Francisco Suárez, *Disputation XIII (On War)*).
2. For an important duty (to the victim)–based justification of punishing the guilty for the purpose of general deterrence, see Victor Tadros, *The Ends of Harm: The Moral Foundations of Criminal Law* (Oxford: Oxford University Press, 2011). For an effective critique of Tadros' arguments, see Kimberly Kessler Ferzan, "Rethinking *The Ends of Harm*," *Law and Philosophy* 32 (2012).
3. Specific deterrence is ultimately defense through different means.
4. See, for example, Helen Frowe, "Non-Combatant Liability in War" (unpublished paper), accessed October 3, 2021 at helenfrowe.com.

5. In response to my suggestion of a wide proportionality constraint on sublethal collateral damage, some argued that such a restriction would be tantamount to saying that someone contemplating opening up a new business to benefit consumers could only do so if the foreseen but unintentional harm to potential competitors were proportionate. However, participants in the business context consensually enter a competitive game in which other businesses might undercut them. They have no right of noncompetition, but only a right that the competition observe the norms of market ethics: no coercion, force, or fraud; and compliance with the law and the general ethical norms of the society in which they conduct business.

10 | Truth-Telling during War
The Ethics of Propaganda and Media Warfare
Michael L. Gross

For a nation established on the rock of self-evident truths, it is probably no accident that one of its most enduring myths depicts the first American president as an immaculate truth-teller. Jumping ahead some two hundred years, Harry Truman confronted the marauding Soviets with the indomitable shield of American honesty. "Propaganda," declared Truman, "can be overcome by truth—plain, simple, unvarnished truth—presented by newspapers, radio, and other sources that the people trust." Seventy years later, the Soviets were dust, but China was rising and no less mendacious. Wagging his finger in an editorial aptly named, "China won't bury us, either," Bret Stephens (2021) of the *New York Times* editorialized, "How Beijing's apparatus of lies will eventually bring the system down is impossible to predict. But there's little question that it profoundly enfeebles the system as a whole. Truth, in the form of accurate information, is essential to good decision-making. Truth, in the form of political honesty, is essential to generating the social trust that is the basis of healthy societies. China's regime lacks both."

So the truth always prevails. But these wars, past and present, are cold wars. What about hot ones? Again, we need to reach back to the eighteenth century, but now to England rather than revolutionary America. Here, in a sentiment Twitterized in 1918 to "Truth is the first casualty of war," Samuel Johnson wrote in 1758, "Among the calamities of war may be jointly numbered the diminution of the love of truth, by the falsehoods which interest dictates and credulity encourages" (Knowles 2001, p. 409).

THE FALSEHOODS WHICH INTEREST DICTATES

War suggests good reasons, perhaps, for treading on the truth that peace does not. The interest Johnson has in mind might be national interest or military necessity. Codified by international law, military necessity "permits measures necessary to accomplish a legitimate military purpose and are not otherwise prohibited by international humanitarian law" (ICRC 2021). For the most part, legitimate military purposes embrace national self-defense and armed intervention to save foreign civilians from genocide, aggression, and war crimes.

There are multitudinous measures to attain these ends of war and most inflict the civilian population with devastating loss of life, injury, and destruction of property. As such, international humanitarian law imposes severe constraints prohibiting all manner of direct, disproportionate, unnecessary, and negligent harm as it strives to protect noncombatants from the ravages of war. There are few restraints, however, on the use or misuse of information. Among belligerents, the law of war permits ruses but strenuously resists perfidy. A ruse, spearheaded by a disinformation campaign for example, deliberately misleads an enemy but does not inherently violate the enemy's right to truthful information because no such right exists. To succeed, plans must be kept secret, and misinformation may help do just that (think Operation Bodyguard before D-Day). Perfidy, on the other hand, manipulates the truth with the intent to violate another's rights egregiously. Enemy soldiers feigning injury or surrender clearly lie. But they also abuse their protected status to attack their captor who is ready to give them quarter. So while their purpose is to gain a military advantage by deceit, perfidious actions undermine the convention of surrender that safeguards the rights of prisoners of war and the wounded to humane treatment.

Concern for the rights of protected battlefield actors also informs what little international law says about propaganda. Here, Article 20 of the *International Covenant on Civil and Political Rights* (1966) prohibits

1. Any propaganda for war.
2. Any advocacy of national, racial, or religious hatred that constitutes incitement to discrimination, hostility, or violence.

Propaganda for war can mean any incitement of wars of aggression (Kearney 2007). Aggression comprises "the use of armed force by a State against the sovereignty, territorial integrity or political independence of another State, or in any other manner inconsistent with Rome Statute" (2010: Article 8). Although framed as a prohibition, Article 20 (1) permits propaganda that sustains any war of national self-defense or Security Council sanctioned humanitarian intervention. As such, the prohibition on war propaganda hardly affects information operations in contemporary armed conflict. Still, one has to consider the limits that Article 20 (2) imposes on "any advocacy of national, racial or religious hatred that constitutes incitement to discrimination, hostility or violence."

No one will countenance propaganda that exhorts civilians or military personnel to violate the rights of noncombatants by committing genocide, murder, sexual assault, or wanton destruction of property. Propaganda of this sort is condemnable because the acts they advocate are unlawful and unjust. Nevertheless, lawful acts of a self-defensive war are the proper subject of information operations. However distasteful it may seem, there are no grounds to prohibit clarion calls to slaughter enemy combatants, inflict collateral harm on civilians, or threaten nuclear annihilation to deter an adversary from future aggression. Credible threats demand convincing communication strategies. Otherwise, deterrence fails. Because deterrent postures, as well self-defense or humanitarian intervention, are lawful and ethical in the pursuit of just war, skillful information campaigns on their behalf are likewise permissible. The challenge for theorists and practitioners is to draw a very firm line between war propaganda and unlawful incitement, on the one hand, and permissible agitation or provocation on behalf of a just war, on the other.

MEDIA WARFARE AND PROPAGANDA IN ASYMMETRIC CONFLICT

To work through the implications of these rules, the following sections consider several examples of media manipulation by nonstate actors, including the Palestinians, Taliban, and ISIS. Media warfare and manipulation are particularly suitable for insurgent groups because they are low cost, high impact, effective, and difficult to counter. And while states may be unable to counter media warfare with manipulations and fabrications of their own, it is sometimes difficult to condemn nonstate actors for their deliberate deceptions. In the first example, Taliban and Palestinian authorities seize the narrative by embellishing the facts almost beyond recognition. But it works. The second example, also Palestinian, is (maybe) hypothetical and looks at the morally and legally (and, ultimately, operationally) disastrous outcome of fabricating an incendiary video clip. In the final example, an ISIS beheading, much the opposite is true. The media images are authentic, entirely unadulterated, but equally inflammatory. The truth, if construed as sticking to the facts, may not matter.

Drone Warfare in Afghanistan (2007)

Following a U.S. aerial attack in Afghanistan's Baghni Valley that killed 154 Taliban fighters in 2007, a local Afghan news agency claimed that nearly 200 *noncombatants* died after coalition forces bombed civilians assembled for a public event. In the aftermath, a number of foreign news agencies uncritically circulated the same account with some reports still surfacing several years later (Leigh 2010). Analyzing the Taliban's information coup, Rid and Hecker (2009:181–182) cite a U.S. intelligence report that hardly conceals its admiration:

" 'Mullah Ihklas coordinated the movement of media personnel to this remote valley . . . and ensured they filmed what the Taliban wanted them to film. . . .' The Taliban commander allegedly directed his men to get a group of 50 to 100 locals and instructed them to tell the media representatives that the bombs had hit a civilian picnic area. The U.S. report describes the incident as 'the best manipulation of the international media using video of the 'locals' telling the pre-fabricated Taliban story in a multimedia interview.' "

In this case, as in many others, the Taliban tie their information operations to images that depict American and other Western forces as foreign occupiers, a resonant and deeply rooted historical theme among the Afghan people. Exploiting the overwhelming hostility these images evoke, the Taliban frequently prevail upon villagers to fight the invaders, resist the occupation, oppose the regime in Kabul, pursue martyrdom, and sacrifice themselves for Islam and Afghanistan. This case, like the next, does not require doctored images, just significant latitude in choosing those most appropriate to the intended narrative.

Jenin, Occupied Palestine, 2002

In 2002, at the height of the Second Palestinian Intifada (uprising), Israel reoccupied much of the West Bank. According to the Israel Defense Forces, "the main objective of the operation was to strike Palestinian terrorist infrastructures and put an end to the wave of terrorist attacks against Israeli citizens" (IDF 2002). On April 2, Israeli forces entered the city of Jenin, a heavily fortified bastion of Palestinian militants. During ten days of intense fighting, reports of hundreds or even thousands of civilian deaths filtered out accompanied by shocking photos of tanks in the street, widespread destruction, and a multitude of bodies shrouded for burial.

On April 10, Saeb Erakat the chief Palestinian negotiator suggested to CNN that some five hundred Palestinians had been killed in the camp and thousands wounded (CNN 2002). By April 12, secretary-general of Palestinian Authority Cabinet Ahmed Abdel Rahman said, "thousands of Palestinians were either killed and buried in massive graveyards or smashed under houses destroyed in Jenin and Nablus" (Brilliant 2002). On April 15, the United Nations human rights commission, with the support of most EU members, condemned "mass killings" of Palestinians and demanded the end to Israel's military offensive in the occupied territories (Kirby 2002). On April 17, in an editorial titled "The Battle for the Truth," *The Guardian* (2002) compared the Israeli operation in Jenin to the aftermath of 9/11. Similar stories circulated in the world press, generating international denunciation and raising the profile of the Palestinian cause worldwide.

But the reports of the massacre were patently false. Despite isolated protests that evidence of a massacre was "flimsy" (Sadeh 2002), the United Nations did not retract its human rights commission report until more than three months later. On July 31, 2002, a UN investigation determined that fifty-two Palestinians had been killed in the fighting, most of them armed members of Palestinian militias and militant groups (of whom up to half may have been civilians). A total of twenty-three Israeli soldiers were killed in the fighting (UN 2002). Nevertheless, the massacre narrative persisted and colors the picture to this day.

The events in Afghanistan and Jenin represent one facet of propaganda and media manipulation. Many of the reports and images connected with each episode are factual but raw. They await interpretation. Here, relatively weak insurgents seize the initiative and create a convincing narrative that can be difficult to dislodge. These and other incidents highlight three critical aspects of media warfare. First, skillful manipulation of templates characterized by national self-determination, historical oppression and occupation, and human rights abuses feed successful communications campaigns. In Qana, Lebanon, for example, Israeli strikes killed twenty-eight during the 2006 Lebanon War (Reuters 2007). Initial but erroneous claims of fifty-six civilian deaths resonated due to an unfortunate coincidence: Qana was the scene of a tragic Israeli artillery strike that killed more than one hundred civilians taking shelter in a UN compound in 1996. "Qana I" thereby afforded a ready-made template that predictably boosted charges of war crimes from around the world *and* discredited Israel's attempts to defend its actions (Asser 2006; HRW 2006). The uproar, successfully stoked by Hezbollah despite accusations of them staging photo ops, misusing ambulances to simulate civilian casualties, and moving the same bodies from site to site, brought an immediate cease-fire (Peskowitz 2010; Rid and Hecker 2009: 141–61). Israel found itself in a public relations "trap" (Pratkanis 2009: 125), forced to face international rebuke or give up bombing. Israel's choice to stand down was reinforced by the diminished credibility imposed by Qana I.

Second, the Taliban, like the Hezbollah in Qana or the Palestinians in Jenin, do not cut their story from whole cloth. Rather, they usually employ a judicious mix of truths and untruths that exploit the uncontested fact that noncombatants often die in military attacks, however necessary and permissible this may be in the view of international law. The United States did not have a Qana I on its back in Iraq and Afghanistan (although Vietnam was always lurking), but no nation is going to find it easy to defend any civilian casualties with the sophistry of proportionality.

Finally, media warfare is inexpensive and influential, leading some commentators to attribute the tactical retreats of the Israelis in Jenin (2002) and Southern Lebanon (2006) and the United States in Fallujah (2004) to successful media campaigns by the Palestinians, Hezbollah, and Taliban respectively (Payne 2005; Peskowitz 2010). In each case, guerrillas could exploit collateral casualties with exaggerated claims of civilian deaths and subsequent charges of barbarism. That these charges were later refuted made no difference. Insurgents gained a significant strategic victory at little cost in men and materiel.

Gaza, Occupied Palestine, 2002

The law prohibiting war propaganda distinguishes between duplicity and incitement, although the line might be thin. The exaggerated numbers and hyped-up narratives by the Taliban, Hezbollah, or the Palestinians hoped to swing world opinion in their favor. At the same time, they also inspired their people to fight on. Did they also incite them toward war crimes? In these cases, it is difficult to know, but a quasi-hypothetical case can sharpen this discussion.

In 2000 French TV aired a video of a terrified young boy, Muhammad al-Durrah, crouched beside a wall with his father and pinned down by fierce crossfire as Israelis battled Palestinian militants in Gaza. For many the enduring images of al-Dura seeking protection and later dying in his father's arms provoked and sustained what became a brutal Palestinian terror campaign. But until an Israeli commission published a report in 2012 claiming that the entire video clip was fabricated, there was little doubt that the raw footage depicted events as they occurred (Black 2013; Caspit 2013). And while the veracity of the video clip remains the subject of contention, I will assume for the sake of this thought experiment that the video was fabricated and the boy did not die, and I will assume that its purpose was to inflame the Palestinians and elicit deep disdain toward Israel within the world community.

Whether the video constitutes an appropriate communication strategy depends upon how the Palestinian leadership and their supporters manipulated it. And here it does not matter whether the video was fabricated or authentic. If used to spur terrorism, vengeance, or, as some claim, "genocidal attacks" (Poller 2011), then it, indeed, violates the principle of nonincitement. If, on the other hand, the video was successfully exploited to initiate and sustain an armed struggle that respected the rights of the participants, then it falls within the purview of appropriate information operations (Harel and Issacharoff 2004: 27–28).

In this way the ethical issues do not depend so much on the truth, if that means that the events occurred as depicted, but on the information warriors' intent. Parties to an armed conflict utilize propaganda to bolster their cause with support from different audiences, including compatriots, the enemy, and the world community. Each one responds to different messages and cues that may be nationalistic or patriotic to the home audience, threatening to the enemy, and couched in terms of human rights violations for the international community. For each audience, the goal of media warfare is different. Among compatriots, propagandists seek recruits and financial support. Among the enemy, they expect to sow dissent, demoralization and fear. Looking to the world community, they hope other nations will provide the material and political wherewithal so insurgents can gain their avowed goals of self-determination. Employing fabricated news toward these ends is not objectionable.

To this point, propaganda need not incite an army toward aggression, war crimes, genocide, or crimes against humanity. But considering that propaganda hopes to instill a measure of fear and distress among the enemy, mainly enemy civilians, it does not take a big step to reach war propaganda that advocates "national, racial or religious hatred that constitutes incitement to discrimination, hostility or violence." Exploiting media for this purpose, as the dissemination of the al-Durrah video clip seems to have accomplished, breaches the prohibition against war propaganda, whether real or fake. To see that neither truth nor falsehood is the most compelling element of war propaganda, consider two cases where veracity is uncontested.

The Passion of the Toys

Is truthful propaganda objectionable? Consider a case sometimes called "The Passion of the Toys" where photographers positioned colorful children's toys and stuffed animals in the midst of monochromatic bombed ruins to doctor photographs of urban destruction during war. Viewing these photos, one may realize that "doctor" is too strong a word. It seems evident that the toys were placed after the bombs fell; they are not part of the debris. The toys add a human-interest angle, invoke images of childhood innocence, and give the destruction a gravity the twisted wreckage alone does not. In short, they appeal directly to the nationalism of the home audience and the conscience of the world. I leave the reader to decide whether the images incite an army or people to hatred, culminating in violence or savagery against enemy civilians. If not, then the images, whether patently false in the sense that they do not represent the facts on the ground or only manipulated in the way of a photomontage, are not inherently objectionable. If so, they remain a legitimate instrument of a just war of national self-defense or humanitarian intervention. This is not true of ISIS executions.

ISIS Executions

In years that the Islamic State in Syria and Iraq was active, social media were replete with images of horrific executions by beheading, drowning, or immolation. By most accounts, ISIS did not stage these executions or fabricate the images depicting them. They were truthful to the extreme and therein lies their force. One can only guess how these images might have affected their chief audience—enemy soldiers and civilians. Abject fear and demoralization at the prospect of encountering such an adversary come readily to mind as ISIS strives to "glorify and glamorize" extreme violence and "to instill fear in the hearts and minds of their opponents and rivals" (Khawaja and Khan 2016: 108–9). Anecdotal accounts suggest that such propaganda works to successfully deter enemy fighters (Melki and Jabado 2016: 93, 98). The same images reinforce ISIS's identity as the sole bulwark against apostasy and evil.

Instilling fear among enemy soldiers (e.g., the "Rebel Yell") and demoralizing enemy civilians (e.g., through economic sanctions) are common and permissible goals of war. So, what is different in this case? Obviously the provenance of the clips is intensely problematic: They are the product of brutal and unlawful acts of murder. Any resulting propaganda is equally tainted. But what if ISIS expertly staged the same scene so that no one suffered any harm whatsoever in the clip? Now the provenance is morally neutral. A staged execution is morally superior to an actual murder. The clip, therefore, is kosher. Is that enough? It seems not because images like this are intended to terrorize civilians and soldiers. But can a video clip terrorize?

To answer this question, it is essential to remember that there are two types of terror victims: primary and secondary. Primary victims suffer death or injury, and their number are small. Far larger is the group of secondary victims who are psychologically terrorized, literally out of their minds. Terrorism disrupts everyday life, erodes trust in government institutions, and undermines human security. Media manipulation, whether true or false, can be equally effective in realizing these goals. And, as this case demonstrates, the truth does not matter. In fact, authentic ISIS images depicting actual murders are far *more* reprehensible than those that are staged.

MEDIA WARFARE AND THE TRUTH

The debate surrounding media or information warfare often turns on truth and veracity. Scholars of propaganda, for example, often differentiate among white, black, and gray propaganda (Guth 2009). White propaganda is true to the facts; black propaganda repudiates the facts entirely and offers new ones in their place; gray propaganda is a judicious mix of truth and falsehood. Gray propaganda delivers the truth, even the whole truth, but adds something other than the truth. Each comes with a level of moral praise or censure. As Truman suggested, we laud white propaganda: "the plain, simple, unvarnished truth." Black propaganda is nefarious and reprehensible. The gray variety is commonplace and, perhaps, the best we can expect in war.

As the cases suggest, however, these labels are misplaced. The consequences of propagandizing are decisive, not the veracity of the message. Some images were patently false. Photos positioning toys among the ruins of war are clear examples of manipulation. But they were so obvious that few found them objectionable on this count. Instead, they were emotionally manipulative in the way John Heartfield assembled photomontages to excoriate Nazi Germany. Among his most famous images are a white dove skewered on a rifle bayonet and a near-naked youth crucified on a swastika. Clearly propaganda, the photomontages did not pretend to be true to reality and, like "The Passion of the Toys," should raise no hackles for this reason.

Assaults on the truth seem to bother us when accompanied by deception. Both the Taliban and Palestinians in Jenin built false narratives around authentic images. With the possible exception of the al-Durrah clip from Gaza, none of the images was patently false. And they were exceptionally effective in shaping local and international opinion to support each cause. Despite the fraud, none incites violence against civilians and, therefore, does not manifestly violate the prohibition against war propaganda. However, it may be that the single prohibition against war propaganda is construed too narrowly. Perhaps it would be more useful to apply the axioms of just and lawful war and examine necessity, discrimination, and proportionality.

As asymmetric and conventional war move away from kinetic operations, one finds some significant lacunae in the law of armed conflict (LOAC) and international humanitarian law (IHL). Neither LOAC nor IHL were designed to apply to anything other than *armed* conflict leaving cyber, economic, and media warfare unattended. Unlike conventional armed warfare, cyber, economic, and media operations target civilians directly. So, it may be that the principle of discrimination prohibiting direct attacks on noncombatants does not apply to these cases. It certainly seems odd to restrict media warfare to military targets when the propagandist aims, as Harold Lasswell explained, "to intensify the attitudes favorable to his purpose, to reverse the attitudes hostile to it, and to attract the indifferent, or, at the worst, to prevent them from assuming a hostile bent" (Lasswell 1927: 627). If everyone is fair game, we are left to consider necessity and proportionality.

An operation is necessary when there are no other means to achieve the same goal at less cost. So, for example, surgery is unnecessary if a less risky medical procedure or medicine is available to cure a patient. By many accounts, it seems that propaganda causes far fewer deaths and injuries than other forms of warfare or conflict management insofar as media warfare adheres to the prohibition against war propaganda and avoids gratuitous incitement against civilians. Article 20 offers a sparse constraint, but it is a critical one that was sufficient to condemn ISIS propaganda or the al-Durrah video clip whether these images were true or false. These cases offer the most striking evidence that the veracity of the images is secondary to their use when assessing permissible dissemination. True or not, these images fail the test of war propaganda. But the others do not, leaving us to return to necessity and proportionality.

Passing the test of war propaganda, many images also pass the test of necessity, particularly when they prove effective and influence opinion as the propagandist intends. In these cases, smart, incisive media warfare accomplishes its goal at little cost or harm to others. Considering harm to others, however, raises the question of proportionality. Is media warfare proportionate? Adopting the standard, legal definition of proportionality is to ask, "Is the expected harm that media warfare brings to civilians excessive relative to the expected military advantages of a propaganda campaign? What might these harms be?" Having already ruled out military aggression and "national, racial or religious hatred that constitutes incitement to discrimination, hostility or violence," we are left with the offending nature of deception. People resent deception and dishonest attempts to manipulate their emotions and corrupt the information they require to make reasoned decisions. Reflecting on the cases here, people may be distressed after realizing they behaved or believed wrongfully based on incomplete and misleading data. Is this a sufficient harm to offset the benefits propaganda provides?

One may argue that disinformation obstructs efforts to attain peace. Given that warring peoples do far worse to one another than lie yet, nevertheless, make peace, this claim seems dubious. Did propaganda campaigns hinder peace talks between the United States and the Taliban, or between Israel and the Palestinians? This seems doubtful. Once an information operation passes the bar of war propaganda and effectiveness, it will often pass the test of proportionality.

On the other hand, propaganda can do serious harm when inflicted on one's people. This was Bret Stephen's point regarding the Chinese. One can lie to one's people only so much. Democracies requiring an informed and judicious citizenry need to be more careful lest the governed lose their abilities to scrutinize those governing. Setting the case of China aside, it seems clear that democratic nations resort to wartime censorship and domestic propagandizing at their own risk and must be ready to end such operations when no longer necessary.

WHAT SHOULD STATES DO?

The preceding discussion suggests that the truth is a *legitimate* casualty of war, not cause for despair and handwringing at one's enemies' readiness to lie in ways we are not. How might states respond? Consider three options: manipulating the media in the same way as one's adversaries, censorship, and changing the facts on the ground.

If states choose to pursue aggressive media warfare, they must consider their peoples' reactions if and when the manipulation is exposed. In the cases discussed here, it seems that the beneficiaries of media manipulation were not particularly concerned about their officials lying. Perhaps they believed the Jenin or Taliban narrative. Recall how Johnson portrays the falsehoods of war as those "which interest dictates and *credulity encourages*" (emphasis added; Knowles 2001: 409). We have already discussed the dictates of interest, but Johnson also hits us with a cognitive claim. Rallying around the flag during war, citizens are particularly inclined to believe government and military officials. Questioning their pronouncements generates doubt and insecurity, the very things citizens want their government to assuage. Proximity to death and destruction helps explain why those closest to war embrace their governments' falsehoods and why those farther away can be more discriminating. On this view, still to be investigated, Americans, Europeans, and Russians would be less tolerant of aggressive media manipulation than, say, Israelis who fight in their front and backyards.

At the same time, democratic traditions most certainly play a role. Consider Russian and American attacks on medical facilities in Syria and Afghanistan, respectively. Following the Russian attacks, the Russians made unsubstantiated claims that the targets were rebel strongholds, or they doctored photos to show that the hospitals remained intact (Hincks 2021; *New York Times* 2019). Following the U.S. attack on an MSF (Doctors without Borders) hospital in Kunduz in 2015, the American military conducted an internal investigation, admitted "human error and equipment failure," and paid compensation (USCC 2016; Bouchet-Saulnier and Whittall 2018). Each nation, it seems, has a different tolerance for falsifying information. On the other hand, when the United States conducted a fake hepatitis B vaccination campaign to collect DNA to capture Osama bin Laden in 2011, criticism was widespread from within and without (Kennedy 2017).

Rather than engaging in media propaganda campaigns, states may choose to censor enemy propaganda and/or realign facts on the ground. In their study of ISIS propaganda, Pashentsev and Bazarkina describe how Iraq, with the support of Western nations, successfully destroyed propaganda centers, deterred ISIS recruitment with a countercampaign to instill critical thinking among the youth, and conducted a sophisticated campaign of predictive, offensive cyber operations to disrupt terrorist information operations (Pashentsev and Bazarkina 2021: 27–28). On the other hand, attempts to censor or block social media sites proved less successful. These efforts do not stand alone but are accompanied by attempts to improve the welfare of local civilians by both defeating the enemy and offering alternatives to potential insurgent recruits.

The ultimate defeat of ISIS undermined its propaganda talking points decisively. Aiming to substantiate an Islamic State's political and religious legitimacy in conquered territory, recruit masses of followers, foster ties with other militants, and emphasize their success against the non-Muslim world, growing ISIS losses on the ground spoke far more than words (Khawaja and Khan 2016). In this way, military defeat would and did eventually counter what had been an effective propaganda campaign.

At the same time, nations fighting ISIS, the Taliban, and other insurgencies recognized the value of public diplomacy. Public diplomacy is a demonstration of soft power that works through good deeds and good press. States offer public works—clinics, schools, courthouses, and roads—to win the hearts and minds of their compatriots and use the media to trumpet their accomplishments. Their goal is to strengthen support for the local government in places like Iraq or Afghanistan while weakening support for the insurgents. Jobs are important, but so are the other elements of human security such as medical care, law enforcement, business regulation, and infrastructure. In this way, public diplomacy counters the recruitment incentives that groups like ISIS or the Taliban utilize to enlist young men (Gross 2015: 213–39; 2021: 185–88).

CONCLUSION

Media warfare, information operations, and propaganda are potent tools of modern warfare. Insurgents and less-than-democratic states seize on media manipulation to drive narratives to enlist support for their war efforts among compatriots, enemy populations, and the world community. As they do, many play fast and loose with the truth. At one point, the truth falls victim to war. However, as the cases demonstrate, the consequences of media warfare, its targets, and the harm it causes are far more significant than its veracity. White, black, and gray propaganda may all be equally legitimate depending upon whom is affected and how.

Nevertheless, states may avoid manipulation and fabrication when other, more effective means can repudiate adverse propaganda without sacrificing the truth. Democratic states would rather not sacrifice the truth as they wage war any more than they want to sacrifice young men and women or expend vast amounts of money. The cost of lying lies not in the damage it will do to postwar relations between former adversaries, but in the harm that may result when democratic governments are caught lying without justification or compelling interest. Thus, black and even gray propaganda should remain a last resort, justified only by the exigencies of war.

Lie-infused propaganda directed toward the enemy, however justified it is, may also fall prey to the slippery slope. Lying to one's people is particularly pernicious. For example, U.S. government declarations about weapons of mass destruction in Iraq or the efficacy of torture in Guantanamo Bay only undermined the fundamental trust between people and their government and impaired support for the war. Propaganda, media manipulation, and fabrication may be soft war tactics, but are dangerously incendiary unless used with caution and restraint.

REFERENCES

Asser, M. (2006). Qana makes grim history again. 31 July. *BBC News*. http://news.bbc.co.uk/2/hi/5228554.stm.

Black, I. (2013). Shooting of 12-year-old Muhammad al-Dura 'staged,' claims Israeli report–video. *The Guardian*, 20 May. https://www.theguardian.com/world/video/2013/may/20/israel-muhammad-al-dura-video.

Bouchet-Saulnier, F., and Whittall, J. (2018). An environment conducive to mistakes? Lessons learnt from the attack on the Médecins Sans Frontières hospital in Kunduz, Afghanistan. *International Review of the Red Cross*, 100(907–9), 337–72. https://international-review.icrc.org/sites/default/files/reviews-pdf/2019–10/100_17.pdf

Brilliant, J. (2002). Palestinians: Hundreds in mass graves. *UPI*, 13 April. https://www.upi.com/Defense-News/2002/04/13/Palestinians-Hundreds-in-mass-graves/47761018714688/

Caspit, B. (2013). Muhammad Al-Dura: The boy who wasn't really killed. *Jerusalem Post*, 12 May. https://www.jpost.com/middle-east/muhammad-al-dura-the-boy-who-was-not-really-killed-312930#:~:text=Muhammad%20Al-Dura%3A%20The%20boy%20who%20wasn%27t%20really%20killed.

CNN. (2002). Transcripts. Colin Powell's Challenge. *CNN*. April 10, 2002. http://edition.cnn.com/TRANSCRIPTS/0204/10/i_ins.00.html.

Gross, M. (2015). *The Ethics of Insurgency: A Critical Guide to Just Guerrilla Warfare*. Cambridge: Cambridge University Press.

Gross M. (2021). *Military Medical Ethics in Contemporary Armed Conflict: Mobilizing Medicine in the Pursuit of Just War*. Oxford: Oxford University Press.

Guth, D. W. (2009). Black, white, and shades of gray: The sixty-year debate over propaganda versus public diplomacy. *Journal of Promotion Management*, *14*(3–4), 309–25.

Harel, A. and Issacharoff, A. (2004). *The Seventh War* (Hebrew). Tel Aviv: Yedioth Ahronoth.

Hincks, J. (2021). Syrian medics lay out the devastating scale of attacks on healthcare facilities over 10 years of war, *Time*. https://time.com/5943719/syria-medics-irc/

ICRC (2021). *Glossary: Military necessity*. https://casebook.icrc.org/glossary/military-necessity.

IDF (2002). *Operation Defensive Shield*. https://www.idf.il/en/minisites/wars-and-operations/operation-defensive-shield/

Kearney, M. (2007). *The Prohibition of Propaganda for War in International Law*. Oxford: Oxford University Press.

Kennedy, J. (2017). How drone strikes and a fake vaccination program have inhibited polio eradication in Pakistan: An analysis of national level data. *International Journal of Health Services*, *47*(4), 807–25.

Khawaja, A. S., and Khan, A. H. (2016). Media strategy of ISIS. *Strategic Studies*, *36*(2), 104–21.

Kirby, E. J. (2002). UN rights body condemns Israel. *BBC News*, 15 April.

Knowles, E. (2001). *The Oxford Dictionary of Quotations*, 7th edition. Oxford: Oxford University Press.

Lasswell, H. D. (1927). The theory of political propaganda. *The American Political Science Review*, *21*(3), 627–31.

Leigh, D. (2010). US forces hit target 'with no civilian deaths'—but Afghans tell different tale. *The Guardian*, 26 July. http://www.guardian.co.uk/world/2010/jul/26/afghanistan-war-logs-helmand-bombing.

Melki, J., and Jabado, M. (2016). Mediated public diplomacy of the Islamic State in Iraq and Syria: The synergistic use of terrorism, social media and branding. *Media and Communication*, 4(2), 92–103.

New York Times. (2019). 12 Hours, 4 Syrian hospitals bombed. One culprit: Russia. *New York Times*. https://www.nytimes.com/2019/10/13/world/middleeast/russia-bombing-syrian-hospitals.html.

Pashentsev EN and Bazarkina DY (2021). ISIS propaganda on the internet, and effective counteraction. *Journal of Political Marketing*, 20 (1), 17–33.

Payne, K. (2005). The media as an instrument of war. *Parameters*, 35(1), 81–93.

Peskowitz, A. (2010). "IO on the counterinsurgency battlefield: three case studies," *Global Security Studies* 1, no. 2: 100–114.

Poller, N. (2011). The Muhammad al-Dura hoax and other myths revived. *Middle East Quarterly*. http://www.meforum.org/3076/muhammad-al-dura-hoax.

Pratkanis, A. (2009). Public diplomacy in international conflicts. In N. Snow and P. Taylor (Eds). *Routledge Handbook of Public Diplomacy*. London: Routledge. 111–54.

Reuters (2007). FACTBOX-War in Lebanon, one year ago. 9 July. *Reuters*. http://www.reuters.com/article/2007/07/09/idUSL0959275.

Rid, T. and Hecker, M. (2009). *War 2. 0: Irregular Warfare in the Information Age*. Santa Barbara, CA: Praeger.

Rome Statute. (2010). *Annex I, Amendments to the Rome Statute of the International Criminal Court on the crime of aggression, Article 8 Crime of aggression, paragraph 2*. 11 June.

Sadeh, S. (2002). How Jenin battle became a 'massacre'. *The Guardian*, 6 May. https://www.theguardian.com/media/2002/may/06/mondaymediasection5.

Stephens, B. (2021). China won't bury us, either. *New York Times*. 5 July. https://www.nytimes.com/2021/07/05/opinion/us-china-covid-lies.html.

The Guardian. (2002). The battle for the truth. *The Guardian*. 17 April. https://www.theguardian.com/world/2002/apr/17/israel.guardianleaders.

UN. (2002). *Report of Secretary-General on Recent Events in Jenin, other Palestinian Cities*. https://www.un.org/press/en/2002/SG2077.doc.htm.

USCC. (2016). *Summary of the airstrike on the MSF Trauma Center in Kunduz, Afghanistan on October 3, 2015*. US Central Command. http://www.humanrightsvoices.org/assets/attachments/documents/Oct-3–2015-Kunduz-Trauma-Center-Strike.-CENTCOM-Summary-Memo.pdf.

11 | Using Hostages in the Grey Zone
An Ethical Assessment
Tamar Meisels

Armies take prisoners during wartime and are required to offer quarter; states are entitled to make arrests and hold insurgents and criminals. At the same time, nonstate actors are widely condemned for responding in kind by apprehending enemy soldiers. As George Fletcher puts this, "Terrorists do not take prisoners. They take hostages whom they are prepared to mistreat for their own purposes."[1]

Recent cases come to mind. In 2006 Hamas captured Israeli Corporal Gilad Shalit, releasing him five years later in exchange for 1,027 Palestinian security prisoners serving sentences in Israel. In 2009 the Taliban captured and held U.S. sergeant Bowe Bergdahi, until his release in 2014 in exchange for five Taliban members held by the United States.

Back in 1947, the Irgun, a Jewish underground group in mandatory Palestine, kidnapped two British sergeants, threatening to kill them if the death sentences passed on Irgun militants by British authorities were carried out. When the imprisoned Irgun members ultimately went to the British gallows, the organization made good on its threat and hanged their British captives, declaring that "we recognize no one-sided laws of war."[2]

Why maintain the double standard? The answer is twofold and arises clearly from Fletcher's aforementioned comment about terrorists taking hostages. Its first prong concerns the status and identity of the captors (sec. 1–3). The second relates to practice of hostage taking and the purpose of captivity (sec. 4–6).

LICENSE TO KILL AND CAPTURE

In the normal course of events, violent acts are illegal and individuals are immune from attack and imprisonment by anyone.[3] The laws of war introduce an exception.[4] International Law of Armed Conflict (ILOAC) grants immunity from prosecution for acts of hostility toward the enemy in wartime, performed in accordance with the lawful rules of engagement. This wartime immunity is granted selectively, to a particular subset of direct participants who achieve the relevant legal status of combatants in war, and to no one else. In order to achieve this status, belligerents must wear "a fixed distinctive sign visible at a distance" and "carry their arms openly."[5] Two further conditions are that they form part of a chain of command within an organization that obeys the customs and laws of war.[6]

Additional Protocol 1 (1977) partly, and controversially, waves the uniform requirement, but only in exceptional cases in which "an armed combatant cannot so distinguish himself."[7] Where distinctive dress is utterly impossible, the protocol nonetheless requires that combatants clearly separate themselves from noncombatants by carrying their arms openly at all times.[8]

Combatants who fulfil these requirements achieve an international status that immunizes them from interrogation and prosecution for killing in war and taking prisoners, so long as they abide by the rules. When captured by the enemy, qualified "combatants" may refuse to answer questions beyond name, rank and serial number, and are immune from interrogation or prosecution for acts of belligerence, provided they are not personally responsible for atrocities.[9] These special wartime immunities are vital because in their absence, most actions performed by soldiers would be prosecutable under a variety of domestic and international laws.[10] Combatants who do not achieve this status, such as Hamas in Israel, remain subject to domestic trial for acts of belligerency, on charges of murder, assault, kidnapping, and hostage taking, whether they attack civilians or combatants.

Similarly, the United States describes its adversaries in "The War on Terror" as "unlawful combatants." The U.S. Military Commissions Act

(2006) defines enemy combatants as unlawful if they do not belong to armed forces associated with a state party under responsible command, do not wear identifying insignia, carry their arms openly, or abide by the rules of war.[11] As such, the United States regards captives taken by their opponents as unlawfully apprehended hostages, and denies its adversaries POW rights when captured by the U.S. Army.

That said, failing to achieve combatant status is not in itself an offense under international law.[12] When irregular combatants take prisoners, they violate domestic law, but not necessarily international law, provided they treat their prisoners humanely. They lack the protection immunizing them from prosecution by an enemy state, but have not necessarily committed a war crime, and would therefore not be subject to international jurisdiction unless they unlawfully mistreat prisoners.

UNLAWFUL COMBATANTS

Legalities aside, some insurgents fight against "colonial domination, alien occupation or racist regimes"[13] while armies do not always pursue just causes or treat their prisoners in strict accordance with the law. Why maintain traditional regulations that deny un-uniformed guerrillas the full war rights of soldiers regardless of cause?

The conventional answer justifying the unprivileged status of irregulars rests on two interrelated features of their identity and behavior. First, by fighting covertly, insurgents place civilians at risk, blur the distinction between soldier and civilian and threaten to draw their stronger adversary into a conflict in the midst of civilians that does not enable distinction. Second, lack of reciprocity—clandestine irregulars do not abide by the rules themselves, and are therefore ineligible for their protections.[14]

This traditional justification for the uniform requirement, both in law and in just war theory, derives from the concern for maintaining limitations on warfare, fundamentally preserving noncombatant immunity. The laws of just conduct in war (*Jus in bello*) are internally structured to operate in an all-of-a-piece manner, so that its obligations are not clearly separable from the protections it affords. Thus, the obligation to wear uniforms and bear arms openly is intrinsically tied to the concern for civilians, which forms the cornerstone of the morality and laws of war.[15] Even Protocol 1, generally regarded as a narrowing of the traditional rule on wearing of uniforms or recognizable insignia, states, "In order to promote the protection of the civilian population from the effects of hostilities, combatants are obliged to distinguish themselves from the civilian population while they are engaged in an attack or in a military operation preparatory to an attack."[16]

Regardless of cause, guerrillas in civilian disguise generate a moral hazard by subverting the most fundamental rules of war, whose purpose is to protect the civilian population by specifying for each individual a single identity: either soldier or civilian, enticing their enemy army to subvert the war convention by attacking them in the midst of civilians.[17]

Irregulars are rightly denied the wartime immunities granted to soldiers because they do not abide by the basic rules of distinction, essential for maintaining the safety of civilians. The reverse justifies the rights of uniformed combatants, regardless of cause, because their compliance serves to protect civilians and restrict the horrors of war. This is where fairness and reciprocity come in: Maintaining civilian immunity by distinguishing oneself as a soldier carries a heavy price—it marks out combatants as legitimate targets, optimally drawing the fire toward them and away from civilians. Guerrillas in civilian clothes take no such risks and hazards involved in overt and identified warfare.[18]

Disguised guerrillas or partisans fighting amid their population (however justifiably) blur the distinction between soldier and civilian, and threaten to draw their stronger adversary into a conflict that makes no such distinction. They specifically defy those rules that lie at the very heart of humanitarian conventions and are vital to the well-being of civilians, above all to the welfare of the members of the weaker population whom they profess to represent.

While insurgents may have a just cause and are not always terrorists in the strictest sense of murdering civilians, they are not legally eligible for the special privileges and immunities granted to soldiers by international conventions, nor should they be.[19] Granting clandestine insurgents the right to kill and capture with impunity would considerably subvert the war convention and erode the protections accorded to civilians during wartime. This is obviously all the more so as far as actual terrorists are concerned.

AGENT-DEPENDENT PRACTICES

The resulting legal and moral asymmetry between types of combatants strikes many insurgents, as well as some scholars, as morally incoherent. Agent based differentiation means that seemingly identical acts—wartime capture and incarceration—are deemed legitimate when performed by one type of agent but not another, based on nothing but the agents' formal status.

The notion that right and wrong cannot always be determined independently of the status and identity of the agent is not, however, unfamiliar to legal theorists, nor is it peculiar to the law and morality of war. Some practices are simply agent dependent, "namely, enterprises or practices whose success depends on the agent performing them."[20] In such cases, determining who can perform a specific task does not turn on the quality of performance or the level of service provided, but rather on the status of the agent.[21]

State-inflicted punishment is a case in point.[22] Private individuals may not execute or imprison, no matter how justifiably or humanely they inflict their punishments, simply because they lack the relevant status. It is not merely that acts of killing and incarceration are legally impermissible when performed by private individuals. Private acts of violence, however well-deserved or performed, are fundamentally different from acts of punishment by the criminal justice system. The very nature of the act, defining it as punishment rather than vengeance or retaliation, is contingent on the identity and status of the agent performing it. This is because private vigilantes cannot guarantee the overall good of maintaining a criminal justice system.

A similar point holds with regard to wartime capture and incarceration. The overall good of maintaining a reciprocal prisoner of war regime, upholding distinction, limiting war, protecting noncombatants—civilians and prisoners—are goals that can only be served by identified combatants fighting overtly.

Beyond distinction and the obligation of overt combat, the LOAC also require that combatants be "commanded by a person responsible for his subordinates" and belong to organizations "conducting their operations in accordance with the laws and customs of war."[23] Both specifications point to a further moral reason for denying most insurgents the full war rights of soldiers. As Walzer points out, restraining combatants, preventing extra killings or ill-treatment outside the permission of the laws of war (e.g., murder or brutalizing prisoners), "is a crucial aspect of what is called 'command responsibility.'"[24] Armies are the type of organization capable of applying and enforcing *jus in bello*, though they do not always comply. Informal paramilitary organizations, on the other hand, may not even be able to impose military discipline.

Discussing the French in Algeria, Raphaelle Branche notes that as early as 1956, Algerian guerrilla organizations (ALN/FLN) issued guidelines requiring their fighters to take prisoners (rather than kill them). "However, the FLN did not have the power to enforce its view on the combatants."[25] While the criminal ill-treatment of Algerian prisoners by the French is notorious, the point remains that the sheer ability to secure certain goods may depend on the identity of the agents performing wartime tasks and the nature of their organization. Upholding humanitarian concerns may only be achievable by organizations with a clear hierarchy, in which commanding officers have the oversight and resources to carry out their operations in accordance with the laws and customs of war, as well as to enforce compliance on their subordinates. Moreover, as Michael Gross notes,

> [g]iven their complexity and cost . . . some of the rules are difficult for guerrilla organizations to fulfill. . . .[26] Guerrillas lack medical and administrative personnel and the resources necessary to house prisoners. Guerrillas are often mobile so that infrastructures are often makeshift and transient. Most guerrilla movements lack the necessary oversight to assure that prisoners of war are treated properly. Guerrilla bases . . . are often clandestine forcing captors to restrict or prohibit third party visits.[27]

Nevertheless, Gross worries about denying insurgents the right to capture and detain, arguing that this deprives sub-state militants of any legal incentive to abide by the laws and take prisoners alive (though his discussion of lopsided exchanges supplies ample practical incentive). In practice, he notes, guerrillas do take prisoners, and the concern is that they maintain their captives' basic human rights.[28]

Observing that "the treatment of prisoners varies enormously among contemporary guerrilla armies, just as it does among the states they fight," Gross is prepared to grant even covert insurgents the right to fight and take prisoners, so long as they meet some minimal standards of humane treatment reasonably adjusted to their limited abilities.[29]

The point about agency, however, means that un-uniformed guerrillas cannot perform the task of taking prisoners, rather than kidnapping, regardless of the level of treatment they accord to their captives. States have undeniably mistreated prisoners of war and are guilty of war crimes when they do so.[30] In the case of insurgents, however, the mistreatment of prisoners is irrelevant to determining the nature of their act, though it pertains to the severity of their crime. This status-dependent liability is not an arbitrary rule, or state bias. Instead, wartime imprisonment is a typical agent dependent practice, whose success rests on the identity and status of the performing agents. Insurgents are rightly denied immunity from prosecution for committing acts of war, including the capture of combatants, because they cannot provide the goods that the LOAC strive to guarantee.

The prisoner of war regime is an enterprise nested within the framework of *jus in bello* as a whole, the overall purpose of which is to restrict warfare. Securing these goods and protecting noncombatants depends crucially on the status of the agents empowered to perform wartime tasks. Privileging insurgency would erode the prospect of limited warfare and endanger wartime civilians as well as prisoners. Moreover, and in practice, when insurgents do take prisoners they usually perform an entirely different act altogether.

HOSTAGE TAKING

Armies capture soldiers in wartime in order to disable a threat. Insurgents are usually incapable of disabling a significant number of enemy soldiers, and can capture and hold only very few prisoners whom they use to bargain for the release of their comrades held by a stronger adversary.[31]

Hostage taking is unequivocally prohibited by international law, unquestionably including combatants and prisoners of war.[32] "The taking of hostages constitutes a grave breach of Geneva Convention (IV). As such, it is specifically listed as a prosecutable . . . war crime . . . No hostage can be taken, whether civilians, combatants (especially, prisoners of war)."[33]

The ICRC commentary to Article 34 of the Geneva Conventions (IV) explains the underlying rationale for this blanket prohibition on hostage taking as "the natural right of man not to be subjected to arbitrary treatment and not to be made responsible for acts he has not committed."[34] In what sense is capturing an active military service member (e.g., Gilad Shalit) an arbitrary act? Certainly, it is not random, illogical, or irrational. Like armies, insurgents capture enemy soldiers in order to gain advantage. "Disabling one soldier *reduces* enemy capabilities while exchanging that one soldier for hundreds or thousands of guerrillas *increases* guerrilla capabilities."[35]

The crucial difference, however, is this: Removing an ongoing threat is the traditional just war theory justification for killing soldiers in wartime, and hence also for disabling them by lesser means, namely capture. Disabling threatening soldiers and removing them from hostilities is an immediate military advantage, whereas bargaining for the release of fellow insurgents is a longer term, and partly political, goal. The notion of arbitrariness serves to explain how this difference in motivation matters, and why the prohibition on hostage taking in Article 34 applies to military captives as well as civilians.

ARBITRARY TREATMENT

As in the case of terrorism, hostage taking defies a most basic standard of liberal-humanist morality that fundamentally forbids the use of human beings as means only and commands their treatment as ends in themselves.[36] This Kantian prohibition further formulates the basic imperative to universalize one's actions.[37] Treating each other as ends, never as means only, requires the United States to treat our adversaries in ways that would be minimally acceptable to the United States, were we in their shoes, and that is therefore reasonably explicable to them from a neutral and objective standpoint, regardless of our own subjective (or arbitrary) point of view or political goals.

When the laws and customs of war that apply to POWs are adhered to, the regime is reciprocal, regulated, time bound, and to everyone's advantage. The prisoner himself is a rights holder within the regime that benefits him along with others, he is accounted for as an end in himself, and the reasons for his captivity can be objectively justified to him. By stark contrast, a soldier who is held incommunicado at the mercy of a clandestine organization cannot be offered a similar justification and therefore could not have consented to his predicament. The reasons for his unlawful detention can be explained—they are not irrational, random, or illogical—and in this sense his captivity is admittedly nonarbitrary. Such explanations, however, can only describe the insurgents' motivation, rather than supplying a neutral justification acceptable to soldiers on the opposing side.

Moreover, hostage taking is not limited by the end of the conflict, and its termination depends on the subjective will of the captors. A hostage situation may carry on endlessly, depending on the negotiations and the "price tag" attached to the hostage (*Cf.* Colonomos 2017, 186–90, 188).[38] Contra POWs, a hostage is not a rights holder or a recipient of benefits within the regime that restricts his liberty and dignity. Instead, he is merely a pawn, or mere means, exploited indefinitely as an instrument toward his captors' ends. (This is what the commentary to Article 34 of Geneva IV means by "arbitrary.")

Kidnapping and hostage taking, just like torture, hijacking, and terrorism, are arbitrary assaults on individuals because no impartial, objective, nonsubjective, justification can be offered to the victim for the depravation of his most basic rights. None of the victim's preferences is accounted for, and there is no reciprocal system that lends itself to universalizable rules. Instead, the hostage is employed as a prop in his captors' project, in a way that is appropriate for the use of things rather than individuals.[39] This is precisely what an arbitrary deprivation of rights amount to, or what it means to exploit another human being as a means only.

MERELY AS A MEANS

It has been put to me that kidnapping of soldiers specifically (particularly Israeli soldiers) might be construed as permissible self-defense against an unjust aggressor. Surely (barring pacifism), it is permissible to attack culpable aggressors in our defense against their unwarranted assault without violating any moral imperatives.

Derek Parfit pointed out that we might harm an attacker as a means of self-defense without treating our assailant as a means, let alone merely as a means. Thus in *Self Defense* "when Brown attacks me with a knife, trying to kill me, I save myself by kicking Brown in a way that predictably breaks his leg. . . . 'We do not *use* the people who attack the U.S. when we protect ourselves from their attack.'"[40]

Are there parallel cases in which it is permissible to take culpably threatening agents hostage, and would this apply to kidnapping soldiers? I suggest not.

Beyond the indeterminacies of just cause (who is the aggressor?), there is a key difference between self-defense against aggression and hostage taking. When I break Brown's leg in order to thwart his attack in self-defense, Parfit notes, "my aims would be more easily achieved if Brown wasn't even there. If I was using Brown, I *would* want him to be there."[41] Defense against aggression implies we do not want our attacker to be present, and therefore cannot be accused of using him. Soldiers kill, maim, and capture in order to defuse an undesirable threat. Kidnappers want their opponent to be there.

This point of disanalogy brings us full circle in distinguishing soldiers who take prisoners from terroristic hostage taking. Once again, removing a threat in battle is the traditional justification for soldiers' immunity from prosecution for killing and capturing. Kidnappers, by contrast, desire and require the presence of their hostage as a means of achieving their ends.

Admittedly, kidnappers might prefer that their enemy did not exist to begin with. That is an aspiration regarding international relations and world politics. Hamas, for example, wishes that Israel did not exist at all. When they capture an Israeli soldier, however, they cannot claim they would prefer he were not in Gaza, when they clearly require his presence for their purposes. Hostage taking uses the captive as a means, and therefore cannot claim analogy with self-defense against aggression, which would most easily be achieved if the attacker were entirely absent.

Consequently, there is no inconsistency or double standard involved in upholding a POW regime for state armies, while at the same time unequivocally prohibiting and denouncing the kidnapping of soldiers. Kidnapping and hostage-taking bear little resemblance to the lawful regime of wartime imprisonment, or to any action sincerely undertaken in self-defense. Instead, hostage taking is a reprehensible form of instrumentalization, appropriate for objects rather than human beings, whether soldiers or civilians.

CONCLUDING REMARKS

Outside the qualifications of lawful belligerency, individuals are normally prohibited from capturing and incarcerating anyone at all. The exceptional wartime license to kill and imprison with impunity is not, and ought not to be, extended to covert guerrillas. Legitimizing clandestine combat, sanctioning hybrid identities of civilian-combatants, would erode the purposes of the war convention. Distinguishing starkly between soldiers and civilians is part-and-parcel of upholding noncombatant immunity, which stands at the heart of the laws and customs of war.

Moreover, insurgents habitually take hostages whom they use to vie for the release of their comrades. Hostage-taking is unequivocally prohibited by international law because it is an arbitrary use of human beings. As opposed to the rights held by POWs, accounted for as beneficiaries in war, hostages are mere pawns or puppets manipulated as means of achieving the ends designed by their abductors.

This verdict of arbitrary treatment is true regardless of whether the kidnapping is performed by states and their lawful soldiers or by clandestine groups, just or unjust.[42] Analogies with self-defense are implausible, because defense is most easily achieved by removing an aggressor, whereas kidnappers desire the presence of their hostage as a means. In the case of the kidnapped soldier, with which we set out, price tagging and bargaining techniques are flagrantly inconsistent with the attribution of intrinsic value to human beings, civilians and soldiers alike.

NOTES

1. Gregory P. Fletcher, *Romantics at War: Glory and Guilt in the Age of Terrorism* (Princeton University Press, 2002), 55–56.
2. John Bowyer Bell, *Terror Out of Zion: The Fight for Israeli Independence* (New York: St. Martin's Press, 1977), 236. See also: "1947: Thee Jewish Terrorists and Two British Hostages," http://www.executedtoday.com/2011/07/29/1947-three-jewish-irgun-terrorists-and-two-british-hostages/. Accessed July 8, 2021.
3. Michael Walzer, *Just and Unjust Wars: A Moral Argument with Historical Illustrations* (New York: Basic Books, 1977), 144–45, in footnote.
4. Jeremy Waldron, *Torture, Terror and Tradeoffs: Philosophy for the White House* (New York: Oxford University Press, 2010), 106, 109–10.
5. Convention (IV) respecting the Laws and Customs of War on Land and its annex: Regulations concerning the Laws and Customs of War on Land. The Hague, October 18, 1907: Annex to the Convention, Section I "On Belligerents," Chapter I "The Qualifications of Belligerents," Article 1. http://www.icrc.org/applic/ihl/ihl.nsf/52d68d14de6160e0c12563da005fdb1b/1d1726425f6955aec125641e0038bfd6
Geneva Convention (III) relative to the Treatment of Prisoners of War (12 August 1949),

Part I – General Provisions, Article 4 (including "organized resistance movements" who fulfil the requirements). http://www.icrc.org/ihl.nsf/FULL/375.

Fletcher, *Romantics at War*, 106; Walzer, *Just and Unjust Wars*, 182.

6. Convention (IV) respecting the Laws and Customs of War on Land and its annex: Regulations concerning the Laws and Customs of War on Land. The Hague, October 18, 1907: Annex to the Convention, Section I "On Belligerents," Chapter I "The Qualifications of Belligerents," Article 1.

7. Protocol Additional to the Geneva Conventions of August 12, 1949, and relating to the Protection of Victims of International Armed Conflicts (Protocol 1, June 8, 1977), Article 44(3). http://www.icrc.org/ihl.nsf/7c4d08d9b287a42141256739003e636b/f6c8b9fee14a77fdc125641e0052b079.

8. Protocol Additional to the Geneva Conventions of August 12, 1949, relating to the Protection of Victims of International Armed Conflicts (Protocol 1, June 8, 1977), Article 44(3).

9. Hague Regulations 1907, Sec. 1, Chapter II, Art. 9; Geneva Convention (III) 1949, Art. 17. Note that all prisoners, regardless of status, are entitled by these conventions to basic levels of humane treatment, safeguarding their life, person, and dignity.

10. Waldron, *Torture, Terror and Tradeoffs*, 106.

11. The United States Military Commissions Act of 2006, Pub. L. No. 109–366, 120 Stat. 2600 (Oct. 17, 2006), enacting Chapter 47A of title 10 of the US Code, Act of Congress (Senate Bill 3930) signed by President George W. Bush on October 17, 2006. Sec. 948 a&b.

12. Fletcher, *Romantics at War*, 109; Yoram Dinstein, *The Conduct of Hostilities Under the Law of International Armed Conflict* (Cambridge: Cambridge University Press, 2004): In this sense, the status of nonstate actors taking prisoners is similar to the status and liabilities of other "unlawful combatants," such as state spies on foreign soil.

13. Protocol 1, preamble.

14. Sybille Scheipers, ed., *Prisoners in War* (New York: Oxford University Press, 2010), 316–17.

15. Francois Bugnion, "Just War, Wars of Aggression and International Humanitarian Law." 84 *The International Review of the Red Cross*, No. 847 (French original, 2002), 523–46. English Version: http://www.icrc.org/eng/assets/files/other/irrc-847-2002-bugnion-ang.pdf, 1–26.

16. Protocol 1, Art. 44(3).

17. Walzer, *Just and Unjust Wars* (1977), 179–81; (2013), 436–37; Michael Walzer, *European Journal of International Law*, "Coda: Can the Good Guys Win?" 24, no. 1 (2013): 433–44, 436–37.

18. Fletcher, *Romantics at War*, 108; Scheipers, *Prisoners in War*, 317.

19. Cf. Walzer, *Just and Unjust Wars* (1977), 181–82; Fletcher, *Romantics at War*, 104–12.

20. Alon Harel, *Why Law Matters* (New York: Oxford University Press, 2014), 51–106, 69.

21. Harel, *Why Law Matters*, 51, 66–69.

22. Harel, *Why Law Matters*, 71.

23. Hague Regulations 1907, Sec.1, Art. 1; Geneva Convention 1949, Part I, Art.4.
24. Walzer, *Just and Unjust Wars* (1977), 308.
25. Raphael Branche, "The French in Algeria: Can There Be Prisoners of War in a 'Domestic' Operation?" in Sybille Scheipers, ed., *Prisoners in War* (New York: Oxford University Press, 2010), 174–86, 183.
26. Michael L. Gross, *The Ethics of Insurgency: A Critical Guide to Just Guerrilla Warfare* (New York: Oxford University Press, 2015), 119.
27. Gross, *The Ethics of Insurgency*.
28. Gross, *The Ethics of Insurgency*, 119–22.
29. Gross, *The Ethics of Insurgency*, 103, 114–17.
30. For many historical cases of mistreatment of prisoners of war, see Scheipers, *Prisoners in War* (2010), esp. chapters 4–9.
31. Gross, *The Ethics of Insurgency*, 119.
32. Geneva Convention IV (1949), Art. 34; Protocol 1, Art. 75(2) (c); International Convention against the Taking of Hostages (June 3, 1983), Article 1; https://treaties.un.org/doc/db/terrorism/english-18-5.pdf (accessed July 16, 2021); Dinstein, *The Conduct of Hostilities*, 227; Leslie C. Green, *The Contemporary Law of Armed Conflict*, 3rd ed. (Manchester: Juris Publishing, Manchester University Press, 2008), 311, 328, 352.
33. Dinstein, *The Conduct of Hostilities*, and Green, *The Contemporary Law of Armed Conflict*, 328 with reference to the Rome Statute of the International Criminal Court (19 July 1998). Entry into Force: 1 July 2002, Art. 8(2) (a) (viii).
34. Gross, *The Ethics of Insurgency*, 120.
35. Gross, *The Ethics of Insurgency*, 120–21.
36. Immanuel Kant, *Groundwork of the Metaphysic of Morals* (H.J. Paton. Transl.) (New York: Harper Torchbooks/The Academy Library, Harper & Row, Publishers, 1785, 1964), 96; John Rawls, *A Theory of Justice* (Cambridge, MA.: Harvard University Press, 1971; 9th ed., 1989), 179.
37. Kant, *Groundwork of the Metaphysics of Morals*, 88.
38. Cf: Ariel Colonomos, "A Globalist Approach to the Hostage Dilemma," in Gross and Meisels, eds., *Soft War: The Ethics of Unarmed Conflict* (New York: Cambridge University Press, 2017), 184–99.
39. On Kant's formula of humanity, see Onora O'Neill, *Constructions of Reason: Explorations of Kant's Practical Philosophy* (Cambridge University Press, 1989), esp. 110–14, 111, 114, and 138.
40. Derek Parfit, *On What Matters*, vol. 1 (New York: Oxford University Press, 2011), 212–32, 221–22.
41. Derek Parfit, *On What Matters*.
42. In 1989 Israel abducted Sheikh Abdul-Karim Obeid from his home in Lebanon. Obeid was thought by Israel to be a useful bargaining chip toward gaining the release of its missing airman Captain Ron Arad. In 1994 Israel kidnapped Muslim guerrilla leader, Mustafa Dirani, whom Israel believed could point them toward Arad's location. While Obeid was

viewed primarily as a bargaining chip, Dirani was viewed more as a source of information. Moreover, on revisionist just war theory, Dirani might be construed as a liable target, as he had been partly responsible for the capture, disappearance, and inhumane treatment reportedly suffered by Arad. Regardless of cause, however, I doubt anyone would argue for the legality of these abductions. Neither attempt proved successful.

12 | The Evolution of Norms in Cyber Warfare
From Stuxnet to Solar Winds
George Lucas

The collection of essays of which this chapter is a part deals with ethical issues in two domains of low-intensity conflict: espionage and grey zone warfare. I've been lucky enough to be assigned a topic that fits nicely into both of these categories. That good fortune comes with some formidable challenges. For one thing, are we able to agree that cyber conflict or cyber warfare is one of the occupants of the grey zone?

Elsewhere in this volume, Michael Gross and Tamar Meisels discuss the range of moral and legal challenges arising in something they propose to call "soft war." If soft war in turn is taken as a synonym for unarmed conflict, then cyber is clearly a form of soft war. In their 2017 book on the topic of soft war, in fact, Meisels and Gross devote all or portions of several chapters to the topic of cyber conflict. Most defense analysts, however, cite cyber as an example—indeed, one of the principal examples—of grey zone conflict.

This Pentagon/Defense Department designator strikes me as a broader and less well-defined category than the soft war / unarmed conflict classification (which I prefer for that reason). The Russian Federation's occupation and annexation of the Crimean Peninsula in Ukraine in 2014, for example, is also classified as "war in the grey zone." But those infamous "little green men" who fought alongside Russian separatists living in Ukraine were hardly unarmed, even if their green uniforms bore no identifying insignia. Nevertheless, with suitable caution, it seems clear that the different experts are talking about more or less the same kinds of low-intensity international conflict, and so despite the occasional ambiguity with this terminology on some other issues, there seems to be no question whatsoever that *cyber conflict resides at the center* of whatever that grey zone otherwise designates.

It may thus appear that there is a broad working consensus that at least some forms of cyber conflict, as soft war or unarmed conflict, are like war (Singer and Brooking, 2019), but just a different form of warfare, and subject in principle to the same sorts of moral concerns and legal constraints as conventional and hybrid war. But that would not be entirely accurate. In fact, for well over a decade there has been a debate raging over whether or not there really is any such thing as genuine cyber *warfare*. Professor Thomas Rid of the Johns Hopkins School for Advanced International Studies (SAIS) in Washington, D.C., has advanced the controversial claims that policy discussions concerning cyber "war" are nothing more than hyperinflated, excessively metaphorical speech. This claim is more than mere academic quibbling because it bears directly on what we are trying to wrestle with in both parts of this volume: namely, what kinds of laws (if any) and what kind of rules or principles or moral norms, should apply to cyber conflict in particular, as well as to grey zone conflict more generally, especially when such conflict fails to rise to the equivalent of a conventional use of force?

Suppose we grant Professor Rid his point that there is, strictly speaking, no such thing as cyber warfare, and acknowledge that cyber conflict is a form of unarmed conflict that falls squarely within the grey zone. Certainly we must then acknowledge that whatever else it is, has been, or will become, all cyber conflict that cannot be classified simply as random vandalism, vigilantism, or criminal behavior is *some form of state-sponsored espionage or covert action*. Usually, but not always, the distinction turns on the agents involved in carrying out malevolent cyber activities. If these are individuals or nonstate organizations, then their cyber activities, if harmful, constitute either vandalism or straightforward crime. If the vandalism is not simply perverse mischief, but is aimed at some political purpose or influence, however ill-defined, then the agents are vigilantes. Incidents and agents of random vandalism are too numerous (and annoying) to mention. The shadowy and loosely organized group known as "Anonymous" engages in vigilantism—that is, vandalism and other kinds of illegal and destructive criminal activity aimed at making a political statement or advancing some political agenda (invariably including their presumed right to engage in such cyber operations freely with impunity and utter lack of accountability). By contrast, the so-called Silk Road was a straightforward criminal enterprise aimed at acquiring wealth for its developers through the marketing of illegal merchandise like drugs on the so-called dark web, rather than advancing any sort of political cause.

This leaves the considerable swath of state-sponsored cyber groups and their activities: the North Korean cyber warriors, the Internet Research Agency based in St. Petersburg, Russia, PLA Unit 61398 in Shanghai and the Cutting Sword of Justice in Iran. The list is extensive and, not to be forgotten, includes the agents who designed and deployed Stuxnet, Duqu, and other malware associated with Operation Olympic Games, thought most likely to be agents of the Israeli and/or American governments. The cyber operations themselves range from exfiltration of classified or proprietary commercial and defense data to destruction of property, severe degradation of military and security operational capacities, as well as ransomware attacks on a wide range of targets, to name but a few. Almost all such cyber operations are technically criminal activities involving trespass, theft, extortion, blackmail, and destruction of property (among many others).

These cyber operations, however, primarily constitute forms of espionage (intelligence, surveillance, and reconnaissance) and covert action, and since 2015 have come to be labeled "state-sponsored hacktivism" (e.g., Lucas 2015, 2017) in order to distinguish them from more conventional criminal activities. Many individual incidents are offensive in nature, but quite a number are either defensive, preemptive, retaliatory, or punitive—distinctions that matter from a legal or moral standpoint only if separated from their inherently criminal features and attributed to nation-states engaged in hostile, low-intensity conflict, and thus operating under a somewhat different legal regime.

In sum, there is no way of denying that at the very least, when we are not merely talking about crime and vandalism and conventional but malevolent cyber actions of those sorts, then we are certainly talking about the remaining kinds of cyber operations as being forms of espionage (or, as I prefer to call them, "espionage on steroids"). This connects any consideration of cyber conflict here in my chapter very closely, as a result, to whatever conclusions we may ultimately draw from the reflections elsewhere in this volume by David Luban, Cécile Fabre, Michael Skerker, and others who are primarily engaged in trying to think through what rules might apply or what principles might be brought to bear, or what moral or legal norms might be emerging in the practice of espionage and intelligence gathering and covert action. That is to say, if there are any governing principles that define best practices (or the limits of acceptable practice) to which nations ought to be held when engaging in espionage generally, then we may expect that at least some of these same rules, principles or norms will probably apply, by extension, to cyber operations as well.

In his chapter for this volume, for example, former CIA deputy director Michael Morell highlights the increasing emphasis within that agency on ethics training focused on enhanced recognition, understanding of, and compliance with that agency's guidelines on permissible practices regarding espionage and HUMINT (intelligence collection) as well as covert operations. As our other contributors attest, even espionage practices can be guided by reflections on better and worse practices regarding the recruiting and use of intelligence assets, deception, limits on the use of false identities, election interference and regime change, and many routine practices in what otherwise seems a very morally murky realm of activity (Perry, 2009).

Many readers, of course, may be highly skeptical that any rules or constraints could be applied to such activities which take place at the furthest boundaries, if not entirely outside of, the normal rule of law—let alone that any moral principles, such as trust, honesty, the right not to be harmed or killed wantonly, or have one's personal possessions and property confiscated or destroyed without justification would find widespread allegiance in the espionage community. "Good luck with all that!" the skeptics might remark. But, having read the profound challenges to such skepticism raised in these pages by our thoughtful philosophers and even practitioners of these activities, I wonder if, by extension, some of the lessons learned in these deliberations concerning ethics and espionage might carry over into our consideration of the ethical dilemmas posed by cyber conflict as well. So, we have a good fertile field to till with these various related discussions, but at the same time, the question remains that faced us with all those things as well, namely, "Can we really talk about ethics or the rule of law in the cyber domain?"

Suppose we begin by considering the incredible, exponential proliferation of incidents of cyber vandalism, criminal schemes, and vigilante operations that began on the then newly created World Wide Web in the 1990s. Early in the new century, most of the nations who were active in the cyber domain agreed, at an international conference in Bucharest in 2001, on a set of norms or rules or principles, mostly extrapolations of existing international law that would guide the behavior of nations responding to criminal activities in the cyber domain. That agreement, the "International Convention on Cyber Crime" (also called the Bucharest Convention or ICCC) specified how the constabulary forces of sovereign nations could cooperate with one another in fighting cybercrime. It also defined what nations are responsible for doing when an international cybercriminal operation like the Silk Road was discovered to be headquartered within their own borders.

According to this convention, when individual governments detect somebody like Ross Ulbright (who turned out to be managing the Silk Road transactions from a laptop while seated at a Starbucks in San Francisco) operating within their borders, their law enforcement agencies are enjoined to cooperate on apprehending the suspects and shutting down the criminal enterprise. In the infamous instance cited here, the FBI took the lead in Operation Onymous, assisted by information and support from other nations through police and intelligence agencies like Interpol and the European Union Agency for Law Enforcement Cooperation. Interestingly this convention for the first time holds the governments of individual nations responsible and liable for criminal activities that originate within their own borders. Theoretically, the right of national sovereignty may be overridden if a host nation for an international cybercriminal enterprise is unable or unwilling to take action or cooperate with other nations to shut down the criminal activity.[1]

The Bucharest Convention thus marked a major advance to combat cybercrime early on in the history of cyber conflict. Unfortunately that spirit of cooperation has not expanded or evolved much further in the subsequent two decades to address the advanced persistent threat of conflict among and between nations and state actors in the cyber domain. In fact, at first glance we observe something like the opposite: a degradation, or devolution, of customary norms of behavior in the international arena with respect to cyber conflict. This is, after all, a domain in which the criminals initially, along with the vigilantes and the hackers, and now the nations who are actually transforming their international behavior to correspond, can seemingly do anything they please, to anyone they like, whenever they wish, with little fear of accountability or retribution.

Interestingly, instead of building exotic and highly disruptive cyber weapons of war as originally anticipated, we have witnessed nations (like China) who were originally expected to build and use exotic and destructive cyber weapons behaving more and more like individual vandals, vigilantes, and criminals instead! This is the surprising evolution (or, from a moral and legal perspective, devolution) entailed in the rise of state-sponsored hacktivism. There are many reasons for these developments, of course (Lucas 2017). But chief among them are the relative simplicity of developing and deploying such strategies (in lieu of expensive and time-consuming exotic cyber weapons like Stuxnet), coupled with the fact that the resulting disruptions, while often grave and serious, still fall below a hypothetical level of attribution and accountability that would likely trigger a kinetic response from the victim.

I have invoked the term "norms" several times in passing, a term quite familiar to readers in the field of international law and international relations. "Norm", however familiar it might seem, is nonetheless a very soft, vague, and illusive term with many meanings in different contexts. In a descriptive, behavioral sense, for example, norm can just mean something like normal or customary, such as simply "how Smith and Jones usually behave," or "what Smith and Jones normally do or tolerate being done to themselves or to one another."

A norm, however, can also be an action-guiding principle, intended to limit or constrain malevolent behavior, such as the principle of reciprocity (refrain from inflicting upon others any actions one would not wish to have inflicted upon themself) or *lex taliones*, attempting to limit retaliation by a victim for any harm suffered to the proportionate inflicting of a like harm upon the perpetrator. Here the norm functions more like a rule to be followed, or a command to be obeyed (or to be disobeyed only at one's peril). Invocation of norms may frequently oscillate between these descriptive and regulatory (normative) functions. This is especially true with regard to international law, which is sometimes described as what (civilized and law abiding?) nations and peoples customarily do or tolerate being done (*jus gentium*), while at other times it is characterized in a far more regulatory or normative sense, as setting forth obligatory (or, at least, aspirational) standards of nation-state behavior within the community of nations (e.g., the UN Convention on Human Rights).

This is, to say the least, a fascinating and complex topic interwoven in law, jurisprudence (legal philosophy), and moral philosophy (ethics) as well as in political theory, sociology, and group psychology. We cannot hope to do it justice here, save to observe an interesting characteristic of regulatory norms in particular is that they are not necessarily fixed or invariant, but seem to arise or emerge in the course of human history and experience (as does their consequent influence upon conventional practices).[2] And this, of course, is the point of this brief digression: to set the stage for an inquiry concerning current and emerging norms of responsible behavior within the cyber domain.

Of course, just as there is skepticism from Professor Rid about the very existence of cyber war, there is even stronger skepticism from most of the participants and adversaries engaged in cyber operations at present about the possibility of there being any really meaningful norms or action guiding principles of behavior. Now and then frustrated leaders and even cyber victims in the international arena will call for some kind of enhanced governance: perhaps a conference, or an international treaty similar to the CCC. Yet prospects for sufficient cooperation among the major players to limit their own independence of action seems remote, at best. The incentives for powerful individual players to constrain their own behavior for the sake of greater security are not presently apparent.

Instead, it seems for the moment that, in the cyber domain, we dwell virtually in a lawless frontier, a state of nature, in which the most unscrupulous and effective cyber warriors do as they wish, and (to paraphrase Thucydides) the weaker and more vulnerable desperately seek the best bargain they can get. It is also interesting from the standpoint of those of us who work in moral and political philosophy, that this current condition is not some kind of thought experiment. We are not talking about a mythical condition in the ancient past before the origins of civilization. For all the talk of the virtual world, this is all real! Indeed, inadvertently we find ourselves immersed in a kind of laboratory constituting individuals and their clusters and organizations in the very first, genuine global state of nature we have ever encountered! That in itself is remarkable in that the actors and agents in that world find themselves very much in the situation that Thomas Hobbes described four centuries ago in *Leviathan*, "a war of all against all."

So now we get to find out how that condition finally works out for all of us. It remains to be seen whether our real lives will turn out to be "nasty, brutish, and short" (as Hobbes describes) or whether, somehow, in the nick of time, some sort of transition out of that state of nature into something more stable and secure will occur. From Hobbes' account, we have some clues as to what that transition might look like, or what form it might take. Perhaps a massive hegemon, the United States or Russia or China, some other powerful nation will manage to gain an upper hand, exerting so much dominance over the cyber domain that they are able to dictate unilateral terms of peace and security to all the other inhabitants of that world. (China certainly operates with that kind of power and impunity on the cyber domain within its own geographic borders.)

That would be one possibility—a leviathan of the cyber domain. Or perhaps there could be something more like what Hobbes himself envisioned for the mythical, original state of nature—a transition to a law-governed civil society within cyber space defined by a tacit contract among government and the governed. The mystery was always in Hobbes how that was actually going to happen. What are the prospects, the incentives, when dealing with an enormous range of individual and small collective actors, each motivated by self-interest and utter antipathy (or at least benign indifference—what Hobbes himself termed "universal diffidence") to all the others?

Hobbes himself was always a little vague about that, insisting that it must happen, it had to happen (and indeed, somehow, it had happened in human history), without a clear hint of what the cause or motivation would be beyond the obvious misery for everyone to remain in that state of nature forever. Indeed, the only thing Hobbes describes as something akin to a moral obligation in the state of nature is to get out of it—to "quit it," as he says—as quickly as we can. So overwhelming is that obligation, as Hobbes describes it, that it confers upon society the right to override the freedom of individuals resisting that transition, even to take their lives if necessary.

So again we might ask, "Where does this speculation leave us in the real world of cyber conflict?" We could conceivably discover a consensus among the various denizens in the cyber domain that we would like to be in a better, more stable relationship with one another than we are now—very much as many (but not all) nations agreed regarding cybercrime in the Bucharest Convention. Especially when, over the past year, the United States and its assets were severely compromised by what certain appears to be, and pretty clearly is, a massive Russian cyberattack. The Solar Winds attack has been described ruefully by some of our espionage experts as perhaps the greatest single exfiltration of information and damage done to vital security and defense systems ever achieved. Its continuing revelations certainly constitute "espionage and covert action on steroids."

No doubt we would like something better. But what is that arrangement likely to be beyond some form of retaliation in kind (which we began to undertake last spring)? Even as President Biden imposed some economic sanctions and other forms of punishment on Russia, their government continued to protest and deny they were responsible, as all malevolent cyber perpetrators do: "We didn't do it. Somebody else did." And it is hard to move beyond that tiny level of uncertainty to marshal effective global sanctions or impose any other meaningful form of punishment or retaliation. Otherwise, as we noted, there's very little prospect for writing any new black letter law or formal treaties, unless (as some of the most pessimistic regulatory skeptics fear) there is such a cataclysmic apocalyptic event in the cyber domain as to drive us of necessity to do that. And the cost of that would be terrible indeed. So absent that incentive, what else is there?

Perhaps instead we should proceed more modestly, experientially, or inductively. One of the things I've been interested in tracing over the course of the past several years, is a kind of plot of the details of successive major malevolent cyber events so as to discern whether there is any kind of trajectory to these events. What, in fact, are state-actors and agencies doing, or what do they seem to tolerate being done? Anything at all? Everything in general? Or are there empirical limits to what is deemed acceptable damage or injury?

And even if there is not anything positive that is discernable, are we collectively learning where such limits may lie, so as to lodge plausible complaints when those limits are exceeded, or to provide objective and justifiable grounds for remonstrating? Is there, that is to say, anything like a gradual recognition of best practices and limits on acceptable practice? Specifically, if we plot time (chronology) of successive events on the x-axis, and multiple parameters on the y-axis to track things like intensity, destructiveness or harm, target discrimination and collateral damage done, successful attribution and so forth, would we discern any pattern of behavior? Would we detect any lessons being learned ("Wow! THAT didn't go as planned! Let's not try THAT again!")?

I start my plot with the first plausible incident of cyber war: the Estonian attacks in late April 2007, and work through Syrian air defense hacks later that year, and on to similar disruptive cyberattacks against Georgia (2008), and to Stuxnet, Duqu, and "Operation Olympic Games" (2010–12). I consider the North Korean cyberattack on Sony pictures in 2014 and the OPM personnel records hacks discovered in the summer of 2015 (that Tony Pfaff cites in his chapter on espionage), and proceed on through time to the massive ransomware attack on Ukraine in 2017 (NotPetya), alongside the pirated WannaCry cryptoworm allegedly used by North Korea on National Health Service hospitals in the UK (among many targets worldwide). One of the most frightening of these recent attacks occurred in late April 2020, threatening the integrity of Israel's desalinization and water purification infrastructure—frightening because this was not simply a disruption of service or a data breach, but an attack that threatened serious, real-world consequences. Thousands of civilians could have been poisoned, sickened, or even killed. Solar Winds (2021), by contrast, while thought to be an enormously damaging act of espionage, at least did not eventuate in actual human casualties . . . at least, yet!

And the list goes on. There are myriad accounts on the internet of individual cyberattacks, lists of "the ten biggest" or the "ten worst." Cybersecurity experts will have a much greater grasp on the range and extent of these events, but it is surprising how much detailed and, with due caution, accurate information there is on these events in the public domain. Tracking them is an exercise that many of us should engage in, partly to help determine the answer to a highly vexed and subjective set of questions. Are there any patterns we can detect, for one: or is this all just random, oscillating hodge-podge? To aid this public effort, I recommend doing something that most lists of cyber events fail to do: separate the operations carried out by agents of nation-states (the Syrian electronic army, the Iranian and North Korean cyber warriors, and so forth) from the criminal or vigilante acts perpetrated by individuals and nonstate organizations.

This is not because the criminal acts are less serious. Some of these are devastating, and often these attract wider attention. The point is rather that our question is about state behavior, responsibility, and accountability—and the prospects for reaching any kind of tentative agreement or consensus among adversaries about what would constitute widely accepted norms of responsible state behavior in the cyber domain, that might just succeed in putting a lid on malevolent cyber operations and keep them from getting out of hand. Criminals are much less likely to recognize international limitations, given that their motives are almost entirely profit-driven and do not incorporate political considerations that might modify their behavior.[3] And in any case, as we noted, we now have the kind of international cooperation, consensus, and jurisdictional coordination to stymie them effectively.

In a similar but more plausible fashion, I believe we can discern forms of behavior that everyone, upon reflection, might agree are off limits. The attacks on civilian hospitals or water infrastructure, that could result in harm or death to thousands who are not properly in the line of fire for state purposes, is one area of prospective agreement and international cooperative sanctions. As Israel's chief of cyber security said of the attacks on his country, "the Iranians should be careful. They are just as vulnerable, if not more so, than we are." That is the kind of deterrent logic that, frankly, makes sense for otherwise bitter enemies. It is all about keeping things from escalating out of hand to no one's ultimate advantage or benefit.

Stuxnet, by contrast, received a great deal of credit at the time and since for being a very principled weapon: one of the most proportionate and discriminate weapons ever deployed, in fact. Now of course the victims/

adversaries didn't share that view, but many others, including critics of Israel and the United States, nonetheless acknowledged that the weapon targeted only the legitimate military target, did no discernable collateral damage and, after some initial confusion and controversy, even acknowledged that it did not contribute meaningfully to proliferation of similar attacks. The biggest difficulty here is that such precision cyber weapons are difficult to design and build. It is much easier to steal some sophisticated ransomware or buy it on the dark web and launch it indiscriminately against the civilian population of an enemy nation.

This tension encapsulates our international dilemma: A few states have the capacity to build cyber weapons that are highly effective, but also discriminate and proportionate, and thus conform to existing norms of international behavior concerning warfare conducted by these alternative means. But even for such states, that effort is complex, time-consuming, and expensive. All states, by contrast, have access to much simpler, cheaper, and politically effective cyber weapons that do not incorporate any effort to distinguish between ordinary citizens and legitimate military targets. It appears from these varieties of behaviors in the cyber domain that the recent behavior of nation-states is becoming increasingly reckless, indiscriminate, and destructive. Therein lies the disappointing devolution of norms of responsible state behavior.

But let me conclude on a more hopeful note. Even if there is no discernable "upward trajectory" in the tracking of actual cyber operations toward responsible constraint, there are some patterns that seem to warn of impending problems—of political affairs spiraling out of control needlessly if they are not reigned in. The cyberattack on water purification systems and similar attacks upon essential, but largely nonmilitary infrastructure (even by criminal gangs, let alone nation states) seems another area (alongside hospitals and health care infrastructure) in which widespread agreement to voluntarily abstain in the future might be attainable. The motivators would include the usual mixture of moral sensibility and political prudence (as most norms are, initially). We don't want our citizens harmed or killed, and certainly not on a massive scale—and we don't want to suffer the reprisals that would assuredly be inflicted upon us if we did such things to them. So our new cyber norm becomes something like:

- Adversarial or rival states engaged in cyber conflict should endeavor to limit their attacks to military targets, and refrain from directly attacking civilians and civilian objects.

A separate issue is the extent of the damage cause by these attacks, in comparison with the military or political objectives behind them. Consider once again, for example, the hacking by PLA cyber operatives of the Office of Personnel Management in 2015. That affected many of us participating in this symposium personally. Our confidential personnel files were exfiltrated. The number affected was quite large: more than twenty million individuals. However, so far as we know, all of those individuals, ourselves included, worked in some way with and for the U.S. government. That is to say, we were (technically speaking) legitimate military targets, not random civilian citizens.

What the Chinese have done with those data since, however, is not entirely clear and remains to be seen. Was this perhaps a demonstration of power, a warning: "We have the capacity to do this kind of thing, and you can't stop it, so you better watch your step." Or are they yet today plotting some kind of major attack on particularly those whose personnel records revealed them to be important—perhaps covert operatives or major senior diplomatic officials who could be extorted or blackmailed in some way? At present, the OPM hack represents a massive attack on a legitimate target, the damage from which has, as yet, fallen within the bounds of reasonable proportionality, with collateral damage to any others limited or nonexistent. Or so it seems. This suggests (especially in comparison to other cyber operations we have cited) another familiar norm we might extrapolate successfully to cyber adversaries:

- The effect of cyberattacks should bear reasonable proportion to the political or military goals for which they are initiated, and incorporate all steps to limit or avoid collateral damage (serious or senseless harm) to unintended targets.

Stuxnet, as noted, constituted a weapon aimed at military targets only, it killed no one else and damaged very little other than the intended target when even when it escaped into the wild, where it went dormant until it self-destructed and removed itself from improperly infected computers. Operation Olympic Games, moreover, appeared to be a stand-in for an otherwise likely conventional attack against Iran's well-protected nuclear facility at Natanz, which would most likely have been extensively destructive on both sides. Many cyberattacks among and between adversarial nations appear to incorporate this additional consideration, a cyber norm that follows from the wider norm of proportionality discussed earlier, namely:

- In pursuing a justifiable grievance, all things considered, a justifiable cyberattack against an adversary (when possible) should be the option of first resort, in lieu of a conventional use of kinetic force.

Perhaps these are sufficient examples to illustrate the procedure of discerning emergent norms of responsible state behavior, even in the face of decidedly reckless and irresponsible behavior. For those familiar with discussions of "justified war," the first two norms might seem merely to echo concerns raised in that discussion. But that is hardly surprising, in that proportionality of ends and the "distinction" and attempted protection of innocent parties from collateral harm are concerns that arise in a variety of contexts in which moral rules are being violated, exceptions requested, and harm done to others in due course (civil disobedience, whistle-blowing, lying/truth-telling, and promise-breaking, to name but a few). The third norm, however, is relatively new, independent from specifics of past historical discussions, and at present would pertain uniquely to cyber warfare, as opposed to conventional conflict.

Might cyber opponents and adversaries be reasonably expected to acknowledge and conform their behavior to such norms? What are people, or rather nations and their cyber agents, doing in the cyber domain that might tip us off as to what we can hope for in the way of norms of responsible state behavior? Such an analysis points the way toward standards and principles of restraint by which we might at least in a provisional way hope to reinforce, establish, recognize, comply, and hold nations accountable for failure.

This, of course, is largely what has occurred in international law over the course of centuries. We hold people and nations now, in the twentieth and twenty-first centuries, to much higher and more stringent standards of conduct regarding the use of force, waging of conflict, and concurrent respect for human rights than at earlier historical periods. As Professor Mitt Regan observes in his chapter, we have better and better ways of reinforcing these higher standards through shaming, sanctions, public attention, and so forth, which is the hallmark of the enforcement of the international norms now enshrined in law.

NOTES

1. It may seem tragically irrelevant in the midst of the collapse of the Afghan government twenty years later, but in 2001 the United States petitioned the Taliban to comply with this convention and arrest or expel all Al-Qaeda operatives from its borders. When the Taliban refused to do so, the United States then petitioned the UN Security Council for the right to intervene in that country itself in order to halt this criminal conspiracy. That right of intervention was acknowledged by the international community, marking the first time (and, to my knowledge, the only time) this new arrangement of holding a national government accountable for international criminal activities originating within its borders has been invoked. See David E. Graham. 2010. "Cyber Threats and the Law of War," *Journal of National Security Law* 4, no. 1: 87–102.
2. Axelrod, R. 1986. "An Evolutionary Approach to Norms." American Political Science Review 80(4): 1095–111. Bendor, J., and P. Swistak. 2001. "The Evolution of Norms." *American Journal of Sociology* 106(6): 1493–545.
3. Although, interestingly, following its highly damaging and disruptive attacks on the Colonial Pipeline and JB Foods in the United States, the (presumably) Russian-based criminal organization responsible for deploying the DarkSide ransomware actually admitted that some of their attacks, or the magnitude of them, might constitute unreasonably risky behavior from which they should abstain. According to *Newsweek Magazine*, "the hacker group issued an unusual apology for the attack later the same day, saying it would 'introduce moderation' to 'avoid social consequences in the future' and insisted that it was entirely profit-driven and 'apolitical,' in a statement posted to the dark web." See https://www.newsweek.com/colonial-pipeline-hackers-darkside-apologize-say-goal-make-money-1590327 [accessed 4 September 2021].

REFERENCES

Gross, Michael L., and Meisels, Tamar. *Soft War: The Ethics of Unarmed Conflict* (New York: Cambridge University Press, 2017).

Lucas, George. "Ethical Challenges of 'Disruptive Innovation': State Sponsored Hacktivism and 'Soft' War." *Evolution of Cyber Technologies and Operations to 2035*, ed. Misty Blower (Springer International, 2015).

Lucas, George. *Ethics and Cyber Warfare* (Oxford: Oxford University Press, 2017).

Perry, David L. *Partly Cloudy: Ethics in War, Espionage and Covert Action* (Scarecrow Press, 2009).

Singer, Peter W., and Brooking, Emerson T. *LikeWar: The Weaponization of Social Media* (Mariner Books, 2019).

13 | The Ethics of Grey Zone Operations
Election Manipulation
Jens Ohlin

I'll just start maybe by saying a couple of words about the overall topic that I will discuss—election interference—and try to situate it before I go into specific remarks. I want to situate it within the overall theme that you've been exploring during this symposium series.

Both law and philosophy have had trouble dealing with types of conflict that fall below the threshold of armed conflict or war, and I think there are multiple reasons why that has been so. And, in particular, one reason for the difficulty is that a lot of philosophers, as well as lawyers, have an impulse that the permissive rules regarding warfare should be cabined as strictly as possible to a very defined set of circumstances. So, the criteria by which we apply the words "war" or "armed conflict" or any of those labels is fairly strict because there's always this concern that the relatively permissive rules would bleed into everyday affairs, so we want to keep it tightly constrained.

Now, of course, when I say permissive, I don't mean to suggest that in war or in armed conflict, everything is permitted, but when you judge it relative to the standards which govern day-to-day affairs, you might say more is allowed in terms of the use of force and lethality, and that's a kind of scary possibility for a lot of people. Now, that framework does some things very well. It provides a tight definition of what war is, and it limits the rules of armed conflict or warfare to a very small set of events. But at the same time, it produces this collateral consequence, which is we don't really know what to do with all of these other conflicts which fall below the threshold, and I think that's very much what we're confronting in today's society, whether it's spying, cyber conflict, election interference, or disinformation operations. There's uncertainty about how to deal with them.

I think there's one school of thought in international relations that doesn't really have that much difficulty dealing with them because some realists and other international relations scholars perceive states to be in an eternal state of conflict with each other. So, they don't really recognize much of a distinction between peacetime and conflict, whether it's cyber conflict or kinetic conflict, because they just see conflict everywhere. But at least for the rest of us who are inclined to make a distinction between peacetime and armed conflict, we're troubled with this categorization and unsure whether or not we should just stick with two categories (peace versus war), or whether or not there needs to be a richer framework to develop these questions.

That's where I think election interference fits with your overall theme for these events. Let me now turn to my theory on election interference and disinformation operations generally. I've been thinking about this for probably four or five years ever since the 2016 election, and I wrote some essays; I then ended up writing *Election Interference: International Law and the Future of Democracy*, and then I also worked on a book called *Defending Democracies*, which also includes a chapter by Duncan Macintosh who is on this call.

In these articles and books, I've tackled three questions, and I'll lay them out for you now. The first point is whether warfare or armed conflict is a useful framework for discussing or thinking about election interference, and the answer to that question is a resounding no in my view. The second question that I tackle is whether sovereignty as a conceptual category is a convincing framework or a useful framework for understanding election interference and disinformation operations, and while a lot of scholars support sovereignty as a useful framework for many reasons, I am a countertrend and I say no. Sovereignty at first appears to be a useful framework, but it turns out to be strangely complicated and messy, certainly from the perspective of legal doctrine, and it doesn't really help analyze the problem. And then the third question I'll talk about is, "What's the alternative?" And my proposed alternative is self-determination, and so I will make a pitch for self-determination as a much better framework for understanding election interference. I'll conclude at the very end with some notes of concern about what my entire analysis leaves out, which is domestic threats of disinformation, which I've grown increasingly concerned about over the last year and a half.

A lot of people in the public, as well as politicians, when they talk about election interference, the first thing they will sometimes gravitate toward is the language of warfare or armed conflict. This was particularly pronounced after the 2016 election, when a lot of politicians and a lot of people in the press said that what happened in the election was an act of war. This goes for Republicans as well as Democrats, anyone who objected to what Russia did in the 2016 election by meddling with troll farm activity being run out of the Internet Research Agency in St. Petersburg, Russia, or Facebook advertisements, viral disinformation on Facebook, and the like.

Many politicians said that it constituted an attack against our country. It was an example of cyber war. And while I want to concede that at first glance, there's a plausibility to that claim, at least from a legal perspective and I think also a conceptual perspective, I'm in the camp that Professor Lucas mentioned before, which thinks that the term "cyber war" is often sort of misused, and there's a lot of things which are described as cyber war, which I don't really think deserve the label. If you look just at the legal category for how the rules of armed conflict apply in the cyber domain, the emerging (though not universal) consensus is that the rules governing armed conflict, whether *jus ad bellum* or *jus in bello*, those rules can apply in the cyber domain but only in limited circumstances, and those circumstances are where there is physical destruction or loss of life or loss of limb to individual human beings.

It's certainly the case that a cyberattack can meet those criteria. You can launch a cyberattack which causes a power station to overheat and blow up and cause an explosion and then there's damage to a physical installation, and it can even cause loss of life. And I think in those circumstances, it's uncontroversial to say that the cyberattack would constitute a cyber war. But often, cyberattacks don't involve physical destruction. At most there's maybe a disabling of a computer system, although even a lot of the cyberattacks that we care about, there's actually not even a disabling of the computer system or the network system. There's simply an attack which has a negative consequence, but it doesn't involve physical destruction, loss of life, or disabling a computer system. And certainly, and this is the key point here, the type of cyber activities that are implicated in disinformation operations don't typically involve physical destruction or disabling of computer systems. This isn't just a story about Russia in 2016. This is a mode of statecraft, which is increasing in popularity, and a lot of countries are now using it in part because there's a big impact for a small expenditure of resources. In terms of manpower and in terms of money, you can accomplish a lot with a very small footprint.

Whether you're talking about Russia in 2016 or other countries, there's no physical destruction, there was no loss of life. That's not the distinctive harm associated with the cyberattacks that were involved in the election interference. Spreading disinformation, using advertisements to amplify a particularly divisive view, encouraging people not to vote, encouraging boycotts of voting, all of these strategies—there's just no plausible way of legally or conceptually describing that as a cyber war. So, for all those reasons, I think "cyber war" is not a good framework for talking about election interference.

Now, let me move on and talk a little bit about the second option, which is sovereignty, and immediately I think a lot of people jump to that and say, "Election interference is not a violation of the rules of armed conflict, but it's a violation of sovereignty." That language of "sovereignty violation" was used by a lot of people in the popular press as well as politicians who described Russia's behavior as a violation of U.S. sovereignty. Also, a lot of scholars are inclined to pull the concept of sovereignty off the shelf and use it as a framework for understanding election interference. They say, "Maybe Russia didn't violate Article 2(4) of the UN Charter, but they did violate U.S. sovereignty."

The problem with that framework is that the legal criteria for what counts as a violation of sovereignty turn out to be very technical—some might say hyper-technical. The criteria are very strict and don't really describe cases of election interference, not just the ones that we've encountered, but in fact any disinformation campaign. What do I mean by that? Well, international law has had a really hard time articulating what is a violation of sovereignty and what is a violation of the principle of nonintervention in a sense. It's understandable that this is difficult for the law to deal with because everything can be a violation of sovereignty, if you describe the protection of sovereignty too broadly. Countries are constantly doing things which have an impact—have an effect on other countries—and that by itself is not enough to describe a state's behavior as a violation of another state's sovereignty.

So, what exactly is the dividing line? Well, it's that point that you can't cross. And I think international lawyers have not done a very systematic job of articulating that line, but the few things that they've said definitively are violations of sovereignty are these very defined circumstances that are clearly illegal. One example is where there's coercion, and that was the standard that was articulated by the International Court of Justice in the famous *Nicaragua* case. If what a country does has a coercive impact on another state—it coerces them into doing something that they don't want to do, not because of the economic consequences, but because of some kind of military or physical consequence—then that's a violation of their sovereignty. Remember, *Nicaragua* was all about laying mines in the harbors and stuff like that.

The problem here is that, whatever went wrong with election interference or whatever the distinctive harm is of election interference, it's hard to describe it using the language of coercion. I mean, was Russia (or any other country that interferes in our election) trying to coerce us? Who exactly is the one that's being coerced? It's not like they're holding a gun to the heads of the people who voted and say, "Vote this way or else." No, it's not doing that, they're manipulating the information and the discourse available to the people so it's a form of deception, perhaps. Election interference involves tinkering with the deliberative mechanism of democracy, but that doesn't sound to me like coercion.

The other avenue, which is explored for example in the *Tallinn Manual*, is that there can be a violation of the principle of nonintervention if a foreign state usurps an inherently governmental function of another state.

If there is something that a local state does, which is part of the business of government and that power is usurped by a foreign nation, then you can think of that as a violation of sovereignty or as a violation of principle of nonintervention. You could imagine some election attacks which might qualify. For example, if another country were to interfere with the process of actually holding the election on election day, tampered with the voting machines or tampered with the tabulation of the votes on election day or even tampered with the process of registering people to vote, then I could see that as a usurpation of an inherently governmental function, because the registration of people to vote is a governmental function and the counting of votes is a governmental function. But the problem is that's not really what Russia was accused of doing, and those aren't the cases that really bother me as an international lawyer. The ones that bother me are the ones that involve social media disinformation. Consequently, for all of those reasons, sovereignty I think is just not a very good framework.

Now, I want to put two little footnotes to this discussion. One is that my answer here is a little bit legalistic, and so I'm a little bit more sympathetic to a philosophical discourse around sovereignty which might, I think, be a plausible framework. It's just not going to be useful for international lawyers. At this point, we need to separate the philosophical discourse from the legal discourse. Second, the word sovereignty is a very capacious term—it's a cluster concept—and the word sovereignty is used in a lot of different contexts to mean different things. Sometimes people use the term "sovereignty," particularly in political theory, to mean "popular sovereignty," like the will of the people, in the sense in which one might say, "In the United States, it's the people themselves who have sovereignty, because that's what legitimates our government." I'm not throwing out that sense of sovereignty, because I actually think that sense of sovereignty actually accords fairly well with what I'm going to talk about in my third part when I talk about self-determination. But the only thing I would say is this notion of "popular sovereignty," whatever it means, is not really what lawyers mean when they use the phrase sovereignty. It means something else, but I like it very much.

Where does this leave us? Where do we end up at the end of the analysis? My suggestion is that the better framework for understanding disinformation operations is the principle of self-determination. All peoples have a right of self-determination. That's a universally recognized right under international law, although the consequences of that right are often under-explored by lawyers. It shows up a lot in the context of secession as well as decolonization; that's usually the context when people talk about self-determination. For example, we've got a colony, it's being ruled by a parent state, the colony perhaps has a valid claim of self-determination. If they want to exercise a nationalistic campaign to achieve independence, that should be supported by the world community—that's the context where people usually talk about self-determination.

My view is that self-determination is a right that peoples have and it endures, even beyond the point when a people enjoys statehood. When a people gain statehood, you can then talk about the legalistic rights that that state has under international law, but you can still talk about the rights that the "people" have under international law, and one of those rights is the right to self-determination. What does that mean in the context of a democracy? I think that the institution of an election in a democratic system is the fulfillment of a people's right of self-determination. It's the manner by which they exercise their decision about their own destiny. They come together every few years, whether it's one year, four years, or five years, depending on the country, and they make decisions about how they're going to be governed, and that is the exercise of their right of self-determination.

What this means is that, if another state comes in and interferes with the process of deliberation, that is an interference in the right of self-determination because in a democratic society, self-determination is actualized through an election. And it's not just cyber-meddling; there are all sorts of boundary regulations that states enforce to ensure that their election only expresses the will of their own people and not the will of outsiders. For example, we have rules about voting—foreigners can't vote in the election. We don't allow someone who's all the way in Norway to vote in a U.S. election. Well, why not? Because the whole point is that the election is supposed to express the will of the American people, not the will of the people in Norway (no offense to the people in Norway).

Consider, also, campaign finance regulations. We have rules about who can spend money on our election because again, we don't want that foreign interference. The Foreign Agents Registration Act, FARA, says that if a foreign power has agents operating in our country, lobbying on its behalf or engaging in activities on its behalf, that has to be disclosed to the State Department, so we know who is doing what on whose behalf. All of these are examples of transparency and ensuring that our political process is respected, and I think covert cyber interference through social media disinformation violates that norm, in particular because the cyber disinformation was meant to *covertly* change the deliberation of the political system. It was done covertly, in the sense that it wasn't someone on the internet saying, "I'm in Norway, this is my view on U.S. politics."

It was a troll farm being set up by the Russians, with people pretending to be Americans, presenting their views about U.S. politics and not doing so transparently. They were hiding their identity and pretending to be insiders, masquerading as insiders, when in fact they were outsiders. That, I think, is persuasive evidence that this was a violation of the norm of self-determination. That concludes the third point.

One thing that this analysis doesn't solve is what to do with purely domestic disinformation. Who cares if the Russians are doing this, or fifty other countries are doing this, if the president of the United States does it directly on social media and pushes out conspiracy theories and disinformation? I'm not just picking on the president; I mean any domestic politician. My analysis, which is really focused on foreign actors, doesn't speak to this issue of domestic disinformation. And I'll just leave that as a question that I find troubling, and I would like to come up with a good answer to it, and it keeps me up at night, but I'm still working on a theory that articulates why that is problematic or illegal, and how we should address it.

14 | Lawfare in the Grey Zone
Orde Kittrie

In this short piece, I will address the topic of lawfare challenges and opportunities in the grey zone. My treatment is drawn, in part, from my book *Lawfare: Law as a Weapon of War*, which was published by Oxford University Press. I'll start by defining lawfare, then provide several examples, including of lawfare use by terrorist groups, by the United States, and by the People's Republic of China (PRC). Along the way, I'll provide some ideas as to how the United States could more effectively be defending against and deploying lawfare.

What is lawfare? Maj. Gen. Charles Dunlap, the U.S. Air Force's former deputy judge advocate general, coined the term a few years ago. He defined lawfare as follows: Lawfare is the strategy of using or misusing law as a substitute for traditional military means to achieve a war-fighting objective. Dunlap also noted that lawfare is "simply another kind of weapon, one that is produced, metaphorically speaking, by beating law books into swords."[1] Lawfare is thus a term with neutral connotations. Just as a rifle can be used for good or for ill, so can lawfare. It's worth noting that the Chinese government has adopted a sophisticated strategy of *falu zhan*, literally legal lawfare, which Chinese scholars have explicitly equated with Dunlap's definition.

As discussed in my book, the Chinese government is one of two governments worldwide that is defending and deploying lawfare much more systematically and effectively than the United States. The other government that I think is doing an exceptionally effective job of waging and defending against lawfare is that of our ally Israel. Who else is waging lawfare? Lawfare is being waged today by a wide range of actors, including U.S. federal, state, and local governments; foreign governments which are allied with the United States; foreign governments such as China's which are adversarial to the United States; militant organizations such as the Islamic State, the Taliban, Hamas, and Hezbollah; nonviolent NGOs; and even some U.S. private sector attorneys are doing a remarkably good job of waging lawfare. Law is becoming an increasingly powerful and prevalent weapon of war. As we'll see from my examples, lawfare—the use of law as a weapon of war—is particularly useful in the grey zone.

Why is law becoming an increasingly powerful weapon of war? The first reason is perhaps self-explanatory: There are a lot more international laws and tribunals than there were a few decades ago. The second reason why law is becoming increasingly powerful as a weapon of war is that non-governmental organizations, such as Amnesty International and Human Rights Watch, are much more intensively raising awareness of relevant international laws as they: interpret them, collect data on apparent violations, accuse countries of violations, promote the strengthening of relevant international laws, and sometimes instigate legal action. A third reason is that personal communications technology and the proliferation of online media outlets have enabled small organizations and even individuals to record and disseminate evidence and/or allegations of war crimes. The fourth reason why law is becoming an increasingly powerful weapon of war is that globalization and the resulting increase in economic interdependence has vastly increased the leverage of national governments, and particularly that of the United States, over other countries and their companies.

———◊◊◊◊◊◊◊———

My book identifies two major and interrelated variants of lawfare, both of which use law to create the same or similar effects as those traditionally sought from conventional kinetic military action. One I call instrumental lawfare: the aggressive affirmative deployment of existing or new laws. This is the type of lawfare that will typically be waged by Western state actors such as the United States and by Western nonstate actors, such as private sector litigators. Instrumental lawfare includes, for example, the U.S. Department of Treasury's financial lawfare against Iran and U.S. private attorneys' litigation against Iran and other state sponsors of terrorism. These private attorneys have won and seized hundreds of millions of dollars in Iranian assets on behalf of victims of Iranian-sponsored terrorism. In contrast, the other type of lawfare that I identify is compliance leverage disparity tactics. They usually involve the lawless, such as terrorist groups, hiding from the law-abiding, such as Western militaries, behind existing laws. Compliance leverage disparity tactics have typically been used by terrorist states and by nonstate actors.

I'll give you a specific example of each of the two types of lawfare. The first is instrumental lawfare, the aggressive affirmative deployment of existing or new laws. A few years ago, the United States and UK identified a Russian ship, the MV Alaed, carrying combat helicopters to Syria. The United States and the UK wanted to stop the ship but knew that boarding a Russian ship could risk World War III. The UK discovered the Russian ship was insured by a British insurer and persuaded the insurer to pull the insurance, and the ship and its deadly cargo had to return to Russia. This type of lawfare—turning a ship around without firing a shot—is eminently suitable, of course, for the American public's aversion to casualties. It's also an example, one of many, of how lawfare can be successfully deployed offensively in cases where kinetic warfare (bombs and bullets) cannot be used, because it's not worth the escalation risk. The United States should be undertaking, in my view, many more such uses of offensive lawfare. How do you get there?

In my view, U.S. government lawyers in the foreign policy and national security arenas need to have their roles changed. Often, a policy maker originates and develops a potential policy step and only then turns to his legal counsel for "clearance" and asks, "Well, this is what we want do. Is it legal?" And if not, they ask how the lawyer can tweak it to make it legal. To fully benefit from the power of lawfare, it seems to me that policy makers need to start turning to their lawyers at the start of the policy-making process and to ask how law can serve not as a constraint but as a tool for achieving the policy objective. Effectiveness in offensive lawfare also requires the ability and willingness to reach out to legal experts outside of government, as offensive lawfare often requires deep expertise in such topics as maritime insurance law, where the leading experts are more likely at private law firms than in government.

Let's turn now to the second type of lawfare—compliance leverage disparity tactics—and how is it being used against the United States and its allies. It's important first to understand how much more seriously the United States takes international law in contrast with many of our adversaries. As you may know, the U.S. Army's operational law handbook says that every soldier, sailor, airman, and Marine must comply with the law of armed conflict and JAGs must advise commanders and U.S. forces to follow its requirements exactly.

By comparison, the Chinese military's Basics of International Law for Modern Soldiers says, "We should therefore always apply international laws flexibly . . . appealing to those aspects beneficial to our country while evading those detrimental to our interests."[2] As one prominent Chinese writer on lawfare issues wrote, "War has rules, but those rules are set by the West. . . . So do we need to fight according to your rules? No."[3] So the United States takes international law more seriously than the PRC.

It also takes international law more seriously than do terrorist groups. A specific example: the use of human shields. The use of civilians and other specially protected humans to shield otherwise lawful military objectives from attack during armed conflict is a violation of international law; it's prohibited by the Geneva Conventions. Nevertheless, terrorists' use of human shields has proven to be a remarkably effective tactic against the United States and its allies, whose ethical and military codes require avoiding civilian casualties. Terrorists use human shields for two main reasons. One is to cause our armed forces to self-impose restraints that would render them less effective. Another is to erode the United States' and our allies' will to fight, and to spur anger at us and our allies, by generating civilian casualties for which the terrorists and their allies can blame our forces.

Professor Charles Dunlap, the father of lawfare, has written extensively about this issue. Dunlap criticized "the effect of NATO's effort to impose more restrictive airstrike rules than the law of armed conflict requires" in response to the use of human shields. Dunlap said, "For the Taliban to survive, it's not necessary for them to build conventional air defenses; rather, just by operating amidst civilians they enjoy a legal sanctuary created by NATO's self-imposed restrictions that is as secure as any fortress bristling with anti-aircraft guns."[4] There's a relatively recent example involving the Islamic State, which used human shields extensively against the United States and its coalition partners. In August 2016, Islamic State fighters fleeing Manbij, Syria, escaped destruction by placing civilians in each of five hundred vehicles in their retreating convoy. There's a photo that accompanies some articles about this event, which I published online, that shows that convoy. It looks like sitting ducks, but U.S. fighters didn't fire on the cars. United States–led coalition spokesman, Colonel Chris Garver, said, "We have to treat them all as noncombatants. We didn't shoot. We kept watching."[5] As a result, the Islamic State fighters lived to fight—and kill more civilians—another day.

So, what can and should the United States do in response to terrorist use of human shields? Well, my view is it needs to look for ways to hold the adversary accountable. The United States is seeking to do so using changes to U.S. strategy, changes to U.S domestic law, working in partnership with NATO, and at the UN. I offer this as a kind of menu of the legal battlefields where lawfare can be fought. In terms of changes to U.S. strategy, Congress a couple of years ago, required the executive branch to provide a report on lessons learned by the United States and its allies, and actions taken by DoD, to address the use of human shields by terrorist groups. In other words, Congress required the administration to develop a strategy. Regarding legislation changing U.S. domestic law, in December 2018, both houses of Congress unanimously passed and President Trump signed a law which requires the imposition of sanctions on various persons and entities involved with the use of human shields by terrorist groups.

In terms of NATO, in March 2019, the Supreme Allied Commander Europe signed a letter to NATO member states generated by the SHAPE Legal Advisor's Office. The letter calls for further measures to be taken at the national level to maximize enforcement of the international legal prohibition of the use of human shields. This is particularly important because while half of NATO member states prohibit the use of human shields in their domestic laws and military manuals, the other half do neither. Finally, there has been action at the UN and vis-à-vis the content of international law. On June 26, 2018, thanks in part to hard work by Ambassador Nikki Haley, the UN General Assembly condemned the use of human shields in a resolution. This was the first time any General Assembly resolution condemned the use of human shields and it did so unanimously, putting the world's governments on record as opposing the use of human shields.

So those are several elements of a new multifaceted Western initiative to counter the use of human shields. I shared that case study because it seems to me that this is where the United States and its allies should be taking lawfare. They need to take this kind of a sophisticated, systematic, and coordinated multifaceted approach to these issues, a kind of whole-of-the-allied-world approach you might say. I encourage you to think about what other lawfare issues, what other offensive opportunities or defensive challenges, merit such a sophisticated, systematic, and coordinated multifaceted approach.

Before closing, I want to focus on lawfare and the PRC. If some portion of warfare can be carefully shifted from kinetic combat to the legal arena, it seems to me as if that should be to the United States' great advantage. While the United States does have more sophisticated *lethal* weapons than do our adversaries, our advantage in sophisticated *legal* weapons has the potential to be even greater. The United States is a far more law-oriented society, with a much higher percentage of its best minds going into the legal field and creatively using law to achieve their objectives than is the PRC. Yet, as I describe in my book, China is currently waging lawfare much more diligently and systematically than the United States is. China has explicitly adopted lawfare as a major component of its strategic doctrine and is waging lawfare in several fields.

It's worth noting that the PRC's use of lawfare is consistent with the doctrines of both Sun Tzu and Mao Zedong. For example, Sun Tzu, the preeminent Chinese military strategist, asserted that "defeating the enemy without fighting is the pinnacle of excellence."[6] Following the communist revolution of 1949, China adopted the Marxist view that law serves as an instrument of politics (rather than, for example, a check on politics and an autonomous, objective arbiter of justice). Chinese law today remains an instrument of (rather than a constraint upon) state power. Consistent with the PRC's sharply instrumental use of law domestically, China engages in lawfare in several international arenas. For example, today China is actively engaged in lawfare in the maritime, aviation, space, and international organization domains. PRC strategists have emphasized that legal warfare should begin, and that legal warfare is exceptionally valuable, "before the outbreak of physical hostilities."[7]

PRC lawfare today appears to be aimed, in large part, at tilting future kinetic battlegrounds to China's advantage. For example, in the maritime, aviation, and space domains, the PRC is using lawfare in relatively analogous ways to advance the same basic objective: to create, promote, and codify international legitimacy for China's expanding claims of sovereignty rights as part of its access control strategy. I predict that the PRC will become far more adept at waging lawfare over the coming decades. China's engagement with international law is a relatively new phenomenon, and it is rapidly becoming more adept. Many U.S. companies now have significant assets located in or otherwise subject to the regulatory jurisdiction of the PRC. It would not be surprising to see the PRC explore ways of using that leverage to influence U.S. policy toward the PRC.

I'm going to close with a short discussion of what steps the United States and its allies could take now to protect themselves against future PRC lawfare. For the United States and its allies, it is critical to attempt to identify and prepare for the additional lawfare arenas and types of lawfare in which the PRC seems most likely to engage in the future. It seems to me that such an analysis is best organized in terms of: (a) which specific additional lawfare arenas and types the PRC might engage in whether or not armed conflict breaks out between the PRC and the United States or its allies, and (b) which specific additional lawfare arenas and types the PRC might engage in if—but only if—armed conflict breaks out between the PRC and the United States or its allies.

I'm going to focus just on (a)—the steps which the United States and its allies should take to more effectively counter current and potential future Chinese lawfare in the grey zone. First and foremost, the United States and its allies should follow China's lead and develop and implement a sophisticated and systematic overall lawfare strategy. Then, the United States should develop a systematic strategy for defending against, and where appropriate waging lawfare against, the PRC. Part of this strategy should involve attacking how China uses state-sanctioned proxies to execute lawfare and other national policy behind a veil of "plausible deniability." The PRC uses such proxies to implement its maritime lawfare, to conduct espionage, to steal trade secrets, and to compromise America's defense supply chain.

This challenge persists, in part, because many Chinese decision makers remain insulated from the risk associated with current Chinese lawfare. It's therefore vital that the reach of U.S. countermeasures, including punitive sanctions, reflect the full height of the parent entity under which Chinese proxies operate. The PRC can't be allowed to maintain ring-fenced entities that quarantine legal risk. Those at the top of the decision-making procedure must be made to reap the whirlwind of their choices. This ultimately requires a level of accountability that is cutting, credible and comprehensive. Thus, the United States needs to change the risk calculation governing Chinese lawfare. A lawfare strategy which creates a legal deterrent plausibly aimed at both proxy and principal could dissuade future Chinese misbehavior and raise the cost imposed on the PRC for doing so.

In addition, it seems to me that the United States should systematically analyze how best to take advantage of, and, if possible, lengthen, its current window of preeminence in shaping international law. As Professor Philip Bobbitt has put it, crafting enduring legal rules is one way the United States can extend its influence beyond its temporary preeminence. In light of the rapid increase in quality and influence of the PRC's international lawyers, the United States should consider how to (a) take advantage of or lock in its preeminence while it still exists and (b) enhance its expertise in key areas in which the PRC improvement could tip the balance of future lawfare between the two countries. My book includes several other recommendations for how the United States could better prepare to wage and defend against lawfare vis-à-vis the PRC.

NOTES

1. Charles J. Dunlap Jr. *Does Lawfare Need an Apologia?*, 43 Case W. Res. J. Int'l L. 122 (2011).

2. Zhao Peiving, ed. *Basics of International Law for Modern Soldiers* 3 (1996). Quoted in Jonathan G. Odom, *A China in the Bull Shop? Comparing the Rhetoric of a Rising China with the*

Reality of the International Law of the Sea, 17 Ocean and Coastal L. J. 201, 202 (2012).

3. John Pomfret, "China Ponders New Rules of "Unrestricted War," *Washington Post*, August 8, 1999.

4. Dunlap, Does Lawfare Need an Apologia?

5. "Photos Show IS Militants Fleeing Manbij with 'Human Shields,'" BBC News, August 19, 2016, https://www.bbc.com/news/world-middle-east-37129408.

6. Sun Tzu, *The Art of War*.

7. Dean Cheng, *Winning without Fighting: Chinese Legal Warfare*, Heritage Foundation Backgrounder, May 18, 2012. http://www.heritage.org/research/reports/2012/05/winning-without-fighting-chinese-legal-warfare.

CONTRIBUTORS

Dr. Edward Barrett is the director of research at the U.S. Naval Academy's Stockdale Center for Ethical Leadership. An Air Force ROTC scholarship graduate of the University of Notre Dame, he completed a PhD in political theory at the University of Chicago, and is the author of *Persons and Liberal Democracy: The Ethical and Political Thought of Karol Wojtyla/John Paul II* and many journal articles and book chapters on military ethics issues. During graduate school, he worked for two years as speechwriter to the Catholic Archbishop of Chicago, Francis Cardinal George, writing on topics within philosophy, theology, political theory, international relations, and economics. As an Air Force officer, he served as an active duty and reserve C-130 instructor pilot, was recalled to active duty in 2003–2005 for Operation Iraqi Freedom, and retired in 2013 as a colonel from the Air Force's Directorate of Strategic Planning at the Pentagon.

Dr. Cécile Fabre is a political philosopher, and currently senior research fellow at All Souls College, Oxford. She is also professor of political philosophy at the University of Oxford, and affiliated with the faculty of philosophy, the Department of Politics and International Relations, at Nuffield College, Oxford. Her research interests are in theories of distributive justice; the philosophy of democracy; just war theory; and the ethics of foreign policy, with particular focus on the ethics of economic statecraft and the ethics of espionage. She is the author of dozens of journal articles and book chapters, and the monographs *Cosmopolitan War* (2012), *Cosmopolitan Peace* (2016), *Economic Statecraft: Human Rights, Sanctions and Conditionality* (2018), and the forthcoming *Spying through a Glass Darkly: The Ethics of Espionage and Counter-Intelligence*.

Dr. Helen Frowe is professor of practical philosophy and Knut and Alice Wallenberg scholar at Stockholm University, where she directs the Stockholm Centre for the Ethics of War and Peace. She is the author of two monographs, *Defensive Killing* (2014) and *The Ethics of War and Peace: An Introduction* (2011), and more than thrity scholarly articles. Her work on the ethics of war and self-defense has been published in *Ethics*, *Oxford Studies in Political Philosophy*, *Proceedings of the Aristotelian Society*, *Journal of Applied Philosophy*, *Law and Philosophy*, and *Journal of Moral Philosophy*.

Dr. Michael L. Gross is a professor of political science and past head of the School of Political Science at the University of Haifa, Israel. He has published widely in medical ethics, military ethics, military medical ethics, and related questions on medicine and national security. His articles have appeared in the *American Journal of Bioethics*, *The New England Journal of Medicine*, *The Journal of Military Ethics*, *The Cambridge Quarterly of Healthcare Ethics*, *The Hastings Center Report*, the *Journal of Medical Ethics*, the *Journal of Applied Philosophy*, the *Journal of Cyber Security*, the *British Journal of Political Science*, and elsewhere. His books include *Ethics and Activism* (1997), *Bioethics and Armed Conflict* (2006), *Moral Dilemmas of Modern War: Torture, Assassination and Blackmail in an Age of Asymmetric Conflict* (2010); *The Ethics of Insurgency: A Critical Guide to Just Guerrilla Warfare* (2015), two edited volumes *Military Medical Ethics for the 21st Century* (2013), *Soft War: The Ethics of Unarmed Conflict* (2017), and most recently *Military Medical Ethics in Contemporary Armed Conflict* (2021).

Orde Kittrie is a professor of law at Arizona State University, where his teaching and research focus on international law—especially nonproliferation and sanctions—and criminal law. He is also the director of ASU's Sandra Day O'Connor College of Law Washington Legal Externship Program. He has written extensively in the areas of international law, criminal law, nuclear nonproliferation, and international negotiations, and is the author of *Lawfare: Law as a Weapon of War* and numerous scholarly articles. Prior to entering academia, Orde served for eleven years at the Department of State, where he received the department's Superior Honor Award and its Meritorious Honor Award. As the department's lead nuclear affairs attorney, Orde helped negotiate five United States–Russia nuclear agreements and a UN treaty to combat nuclear terrorism. His work has been featured in leading outlets including the *Wall Street Journal*, the *Washington Post*, and *Foreign Affairs*. He has done on-air commentary for networks and stations including NBC, ABC, Fox, PBS, and Al Jazeera.

Dr. David Luban is a university professor and professor of law and philosophy at Georgetown Law. Since 2013, he has also served as Class of 1984 Distinguished Chair in Ethics at the U.S. Naval Academy's Stockdale Center for Ethical Leadership. His research interests center on moral and legal responsibility in organizational settings, including law firms, government, and the military. In addition to legal ethics, he writes on international criminal law, national security, and just war theory. His current project is a book on the moral and legal philosophy of Hannah Arendt. Luban is a member of the American Academy of Arts and Sciences. He has been a Guggenheim Fellow and a Fellow of the Woodrow Wilson Center, and has received prizes for distinguished scholarship from the American Bar Foundation and the New York State Bar Association. In 2011 he was a Fellow of the Institute for Advanced Studies at Hebrew University. His books include *Lawyers and Justice: An Ethical Study* (1988), *Legal Modernism* (1994), and *Legal Ethics and Human Dignity* (2007). His most recent book, *Torture, Power, and Law* (2014), won the American Publishers Association PROSE Award for professional and scholarly excellence in philosophy. Other books include edited anthologies and casebooks on international criminal law and legal ethics. Along with many scholarly articles, Luban has written for the *Boston Review*, the *New York Review of Books*, and *Slate*.

Dr. George Lucas is Professor Emeritus at the U.S. Naval Academy and Naval Postgraduate School and currently serves as a Senior Fellow at the Stockdale Center for Ethical Leadership at the Naval Academy. He is the editor of *Routledge Handbook of Military Ethics* (2015), and his monographs include *Ethics and Military Strategy in the 21st Century: Moving beyond Clausewitz* (2020), *Ethics and Cyber Warfare* (2017), and *Military Ethics: What Everyone Needs to Know* (2016).

Dr. Tamar Meisels is a political theorist and professor at The School of Political Science, Government and International Relations, Tel-Aviv University. She is the author of *Territorial Rights* (2005 and 2009), *The Trouble with Terror: Liberty, Security and the Response to Terrorism* (2008), *Contemporary Just War: Theory and Practice* (2017), and coeditor (with Michael L. Gross) of *Soft War: The Ethics of Unarmed Conflict* (2017).

During his thirty-three-year career with the Central Intelligence Agency, **Michael Morell** served as its deputy director from 2010 to 2013, and twice as its acting director: first in 2011, and then from 2012 to 2013. As a CIA analyst, he served as presidential daily briefer to George W. Bush, including on the morning of 9/11. He is the author of *The Great War of Our Time: The CIA's Fight against Terrorism from Al Qa'ida to ISIS*, an on-air contributor on intelligence and national security for CBS, a contributing columnist to the *Washington Post*, and a senior counselor and the global chairman of the Geo-Political Risk Practice at Beacon Global Strategies LLC.

Dr. Jens Ohlin is the Allan R. Tessler Dean of Cornell Law School. He holds a PhD from Columbia University and a JD from Columbia Law School, and his scholarly work stands at the intersection of four related fields: criminal law, criminal procedure, public international law, and the laws of war. His latest books include *Election Interference: International Law and the Future of Democracy* (2020), *Criminal Procedure: Doctrine, Application, and Practice* (2019), *Criminal Law: Doctrine, Application, and Practice* (2nd ed., 2018), *International Law: Evolving Doctrine and Practice* (2018), *Necessity in International Law* (2016) (with Larry May), and *The Assault on International Law* (2015). He is coeditor of the Oxford Series in Ethics, National Security, and the Rule of Law.

Professor Sir David Omand was the first UK security and intelligence coordinator, responsible to the prime minister for the professional health of the intelligence community, national counter-terrorism strategy, and homeland security. He served for seven years on the Joint Intelligence Committee. He was permanent secretary of the Home Office from 1997 to 2000, and before that director of GCHQ (the UK Sigint Agency). Previously in the

Ministry of Defence as deputy under secretary of state for policy, he was particularly concerned with long term strategy with the British military contribution in restoring peace in the former Yugoslavia and the recasting of British nuclear deterrence policy at the end of the Cold War. He was principal private secretary to the defense secretary during the Falklands conflict, and served for three years in NATO Brussels as the UK defense counselor. He has been a visiting professor in the Department of War Studies since 2005–2006. He is the coauthor of *Principled Spying: The Ethics of Secret Intelligence* (2018), and his latest book is *How Spies Think: 10 Lessons from Intelligence* (2020).

Dr. C. Anthony Pfaff is Research Professor for Strategy, the Military Profession, and Ethic at the Strategic Studies Institute (SSI), U.S. Army War College, Carlisle, Pennsylvania, and a Senior Nonresident Fellow at the Atlantic Council. A retired Army colonel and Foreign Area Officer (FAO) for the Middle East and North Africa, Dr. Pfaff recently served as director for Iraq on the National Security Council Staff. His last active duty posting was senior Army and military advisor to the State Department from 2013 to 2016, where he served on the Policy Planning Staff advising on cyber, regional military affairs, the Arab Gulf Region, Iran, and security sector assistance reform. Prior to taking the State Department position, he served as the defense attaché in Baghdad, the chief of international military affairs for U.S. Army Central Command, and as the defense attaché in Kuwait. He served twice in Operation Iraqi Freedom, and also served as the senior intelligence officer on the Iraq Intelligence Working Group and as a UN observer along the Iraq-Kuwait border. Prior to becoming a FAO, Dr. Pfaff was on the faculty at West Point as an assistant professor of philosophy. As a company grade Army officer, he deployed to Operation Desert Shield and Desert Storm with 82nd Airborne Division and participated in Operation Able Sentry with the 1st Armored Division. Dr. Pfaff has a master's degree in philosophy from Stanford University and a doctorate in philosophy from Georgetown University. He is the author of numerous articles in professional and scholarly publications.

Mitt Regan is McDevitt Professor of Jurisprudence and co-director of the Center for the Study of the Legal Profession at Georgetown University Law Center. He is also adjunct faculty member at the Center for Military and Security Law at the Australian National University College of Law, and an international research fellow at the University of Oxford's Centre for Professional Service Firms. His work focuses on organizational, cultural, and psychological aspects of ethical issues in business, law practice, and the national security and military settings. He is the author of *Eat What You Kill: The Fall of a Wall Street Lawyer* and coauthor of *Confidence Games: Lawyers, Accountants, and the Tax Shelter Industry* and *Legal Ethics in Corporate Practice*. Professor Regan served as law clerk to Justice William J. Brennan Jr. on the U.S. Supreme Court and then-Judge Ruth Bader Ginsburg on the U.S. Court of Appeals for the D.C. Circuit.

Dr. Michael Skerker is a professor in the Department of Leadership, Ethics, and Law at the U.S. Naval Academy. His academic interests include professional ethics, just war theory, moral pluralism, theological ethics, and militant jihadism. Publications include articles and chapters on ethics and asymmetrical war, collective responsibility, police ethics, intelligence ethics, and two monographs: *An Ethics of Interrogation* (2010) and *The Moral Status of Combatants: A New Theory* (2020). Professor Skerker is also the coeditor of *Sovereignty, and the New Executive Authority* and *Military Virtues* (2019).

ABOUT THE STOCKDALE CENTER

For over a century and a half, the U.S. Naval Academy has served as a beacon of moral and ethical leadership to the nation and to the world—producing leaders of uncompromising character, who have fought our wars with honor and have gone on to serve as positive role models on a global stage.

In response to an ever-changing world and the imperative to enhance the development of ethical leaders, the Secretary of the Navy established the Center for the Study of Professional Military Ethics at the U.S. Naval Academy in 1998. Building on the Academy's track record of developing some of the nation's finest leaders, the Navy chartered the Center to reach out to not only the Naval Academy, but also to the wider audience of the Navy, Marine Corps, and the nation at large. Over the years, the vision has expanded to transforming ethical leadership development worldwide. In 2006, the Center was given a new name—The Vice Admiral James B. Stockdale Center for Ethical Leadership. The Center has continued to refocus and refine its mission, which is to empower leaders to make courageous ethical decisions.

Vice Admiral Stockdale—a member of the Class of 1947, a prisoner of war for seven and a half years (four of which were in solitary confinement), a recipient of the Medal of Honor, and a lifelong student of philosophy, ethics, and leadership—embodied the selfless and courageous leadership sought in midshipmen, officers, and national leaders.

The Naval Institute Press is the book-publishing arm of the U.S. Naval Institute, a private, nonprofit, membership society for sea service professionals and others who share an interest in naval and maritime affairs. Established in 1873 at the U.S. Naval Academy in Annapolis, Maryland, where its offices remain today, the Naval Institute has members worldwide.

Members of the Naval Institute support the education programs of the society and receive the influential monthly magazine *Proceedings* or the colorful bimonthly magazine *Naval History* and discounts on fine nautical prints and on ship and aircraft photos. They also have access to the transcripts of the Institute's Oral History Program and get discounted admission to any of the Institute-sponsored seminars offered around the country.

The Naval Institute's book-publishing program, begun in 1898 with basic guides to naval practices, has broadened its scope to include books of more general interest. Now the Naval Institute Press publishes about seventy titles each year, ranging from how-to books on boating and navigation to battle histories, biographies, ship and aircraft guides, and novels. Institute members receive significant discounts on the Press' more than eight hundred books in print.

Full-time students are eligible for special half-price membership rates. Life memberships are also available.

For more information about Naval Institute Press books that are currently available, visit www.usni.org/press/books. To learn about joining the U.S. Naval Institute, please write to:

Member Services
U.S. Naval Institute
291 Wood Road
Annapolis, MD 21402-5034
Telephone: (800) 233-8764
Fax: (410) 571-1703
Web address: www.usni.org

www.ingramcontent.com/pod-product-compliance
Ingram Content Group UK Ltd.
Pitfield, Milton Keynes, MK11 3LW, UK
UKHW041919140426
5217IPUK00013B/232